# RAPTORS
## ON THE
# FLAMBEAU

### BOOK TWO:

*Teen Years*

## T.L. HERSHEY

NEWMAN SPRINGS PUBLISHING
320 Broad Street
Red Bank, NJ 07701

First originally published by Newman Springs Publishing 2020

Cover artwork by Talia Brinker

ISBN 978-1-64801-774-2 (Paperback)
ISBN 978-1-64801-775-9 (Digital)

Printed in the United States of America

# DEDICATION

To Johnny Raptor.

# CONTENTS

# FOREWORD

Many of you struggled through a painful childhood with the Raptor boys in book one—*The Cradle of the Raptor.*

This book finds the family moving to a new state and a whole new set of social and economic dynamics! I would emphasize again that life is experienced by perspective, and most of the perspective in this book is shared as I saw it as I struggled to adjust to a normal society and lifestyle in our new world. I would ask my readers to remember that we all have shortcomings, and my parents were not much different from many other parents of that day in spite of how I viewed them. In the final analysis, we are all works in progress!

—*Michael Raptor*

# PROLOGUE

He pulled the big red 4×4 Ram pickup truck to the parking curb in front of the convenience store and switched off the diesel engine. He was a big man who was slowly losing ground in the battle of health and aging. The same could not be said for the high-voltage little boy strapped securely into the child safety seat in the Ram's rear seat. "Grandpa," he instructed, "you can come and get me out, but I will walk in by myself!"

Michael spent a long minute locking eyes in the rearview mirror with the imperious little three-year-old boy in the backseat. Since he owned his own business, he was able to make time each week to take the little guy out for lunch to a place of his choosing. Usually it would be incorporated into a run somewhere for business supplies. Today they were eating Hot Stuff pizza at a convenience store.

Michael walked around the cab and unbelted the tyke who squirmed to the ground and headed inside. The boy was small for his age, but he never let that hinder his life's mission of instructing everyone around him in exactly how he wanted them to perform. Once in a building supply store, he was hounding his father for a toy when his father told him that it was "too expensive and exceeded his budget," to which he forcefully replied, "I don't have a budget!"

Inside the store, Michael selected a pizza while his grandson opened the big wall cooler and selected a cold Kool-Aid-type drink from the large wall cooler.

About halfway through their meal, the little fellow decided he would rather have some of grandpa's pop. He set his half-empty juice bottle on the table and said, "Grandpa, I want some of your pop!"

"Well," his grandfather responded, "I will be happy to share my drink with you after you have finished yours, but if you start drinking mine now, the rest of yours will go to waste."

"I want pop *now*," he clarified.

"And I just explained to you why you have to finish your drink first," his grandfather replied. "Waste not, want not, that's what the Bible says!" He felt an immediate twinge of guilt for taking so much literary license with scriptural paraphrase and lamely added, "Or something like that!"

From across the table, the little fellow regarded him with an unblinking stare. He had immediately picked up on his grandfather's uncertainty and was about to set the record straight and move in for the kill. When he spoke, his voice was concise and authoritative. "The Bible says *pop!*"

Michael laughed out loud! This little guy was so much like him at that age. He was as close to his son, the boy's father, as it is possible for a father and son to be, but his son had grown up with a gentle and considerate nature, always sensitive to the needs of others. His son's son, though, was a throwback to the grandfather—forceful and aggressive, not giving much thought to other people's" agendas as they pursued their own.

Michael's thoughts drifted back in time to a rough childhood on a dusty Indian reservation. Pop there had been a rare and wonderful treat. A nickel would buy a sixteen-ounce glass bottle of the delicious beverage. It had been a tiny bright spot in a long dark existence. But then life had radically changed!

Blessed is he who has a sense of humor for it
is life's great shock absorber!

*(Author Unknown)*

# HORSES AND
# HOUSE DOORS

*1968*

The robin-egg blue Dodge pickup rumbled into dawn of a beautiful Ohio morning. The two riding horses on the bed were shifting restlessly. They had endured the long ride from South Dakota with only occasional stops for fuel and rest breaks. Their hay bags were nearly empty, and their water rations had been limited after Twinkle, the glossy black mare, had lifted her tail and shot out a yellow gusher of urine, which nearly splashed on the battered, old Chevy car following them to their new world. The pickup hauling the horses had been the subject of many curious and amused looks as they traveled east. The driver and proud owner was a handsome and powerfully built man named Carl Raptor. He was not only proud of the half-ton Dodge pickup with the slant six engine, but the rack containing the horses was his own personal design. Thrift had been the order of his entire life, so when he had needed a rack to haul his beloved horses to their new home in Ohio, he had collected some rusty and not very straight pipe and had the local welding shop build the rack to his specifications. The local welding shop was actually only a neighbor who had an ancient welder in his tumbledown shed. The shed was crammed from wall to wall with assorted junk, making it barely possible to walk through it, so the welder was conveniently located near the door where the cables could be strung outside to practice his "craft." His work was something to behold—unsightly blobs of weld intermittently spaced along the surface to be joined. Given his inability to maintain a consistent welding bead, his policy was to keep piling up the weld until there was a reasonable chance that it would hold. The result looked very similar to the ground under a chicken roost. But quality was never a big concern with Carl Raptor. He now had his rack to fit on his pickup, which he had bought with the proceeds from the sale of their farm and possessions.

Between the cab of the truck and the front of the rack, Carl had tied two old house doors to block the wind for the horses. Somehow it never occurred to him to cut the doors down, so they protruded oddly several feet above the hideous rack. The weird ensemble was redeemed somewhat by the two handsome horses on board. Dusty, the compact buckskin quarter horse, was the color of buttermilk with a black mane and tail. His tail, though, was only a wispy remnant of the long and luxurious glossy black tail he had once had. Running half-wild on the reservation farm where the Raptors had lived for thirteen years, the horses' manes and tails were magnets for the cockleburs which turned them into ugly matted ropes. The easiest way to deal with the problem was to simply cut off the matted hair and let it grow back. But when Carl had cut Dusty's matted tail, he had cut it too short, in effect "docking" the tail which precluded regrowth. Randy, Carl's second eldest son, was actually the official owner of Dusty, and he had protested the hair cutting, but in the Raptor household, Carl was god, and protestations were mild and short-lived unless you wanted to risk a few blows from god's hand to your face.

The other horse, "Twinkle," was slightly taller and leaner than Dusty. She was jet-black with two white socks and a star on her face. Of the many horses that had come and gone on the Raptor farm over the years, these were two of the best. The rest had all been sold off with the milk cows at the auction before they left. Twinkle was jointly owned by Carl and his third son, Michael, who was riding in the old Chevy following the pickup. Carl's wife Charlotte was driving the car and her three youngest sons Michael, Johnny, and Eli the toddler were packed in with her among the personal possessions headed for their new home in Ohio. The two eldest boys, Carl Jr. and Randy, were riding with Carl in the pickup.

Michael woke from his catnap to the sound of the Chevy rumbling across a large bridge spanning the mighty Flambeau river in Rock County, Ohio.

"We're almost there," Charlotte announced cheerfully, despite the fatigue visible on her face. Stopping at motels to rest was simply not in their budget, and she and her husband had needed to make do with several naps at roadside rest areas. But Charlotte was made of strong stuff and had dealt with situations on the reservation farm that would have made many a man quake with fear.

Michael gazed out the window with increasing interest as the scenery flowed by. They were driving on a county road which was winding along beside a large, fast-flowing river called the Flambeau.

Finally, the blue pickup turned right into a long gravel lane, which wound around to a very large and very decrepit clapboard house with a sagging porch and peeling white paint. Not far behind the house was the woods bordering the river, and on either side were overgrown hayfields. There were no real shade trees near the house, and the lawn was overgrown with weeds and borders impossible to define. Dark old-fashioned large windows stared out over the unkept lawn giving the house a brooding, even sinister appearance.

Charlotte backed the old Chevy up to the sagging porch and switched off the engine. Michael climbed out stiffly and looked around. He saw his father pull the blue pick up over beside the tired looking shed and shut off the engine. He wondered what they were going to do with the horses. There was not an inch of fence on the entire property as far as he could see, although there was plenty of grass. Charlotte was soon busy dragging boxes and cartons of possessions into the house from the trunk of the car and issuing instructions like a drill sergeant. Michael obeyed reluctantly, carrying in their battered possessions all the while watching out the corner of his eye to see what was happening with the truck and its precious cargo. He saw his father stroll around the grounds, looking for something in the tall grass, and wondered what he was searching for. He appeared to find it sometime later and climbed back into the driver's seat of the pickup and drove it through the tall grass until the back tires dropped down into a fairly deep gully. This brought the ground behind the pickup much closer to the pickup bed, and after shoveling some dirt up against the bumper, they finally were able to back the horses off of the pickup. The horses seemed relieved for more reasons than one, and as soon as they had accommodated their bathroom needs, they went to work chomping the tall grass hungrily.

"We are going to need to get some fence made right away," Carl commented to the older boys. "Until then you boys will have to take turns grazing the horses on lead ropes."

While most people assume horses can simply be tied out to graze on a long rope, that is not the case unless they have been taught to picket. Horses become confused and excited when they have a long rope and think they are free until they hit the end of the rope with a jerk which scares them, and they tend to overreact. They must also learn how to step over and around the picket rope, so it doesn't tangle their feet and create serious rope burns or even injuries by tripping them to the ground. Teaching horses to picket was not something Carl had done much in his life. He would much rather build electric fence and let them roam inside the fenced off pasture. Until he could get some fence made, the horses would be tied in the tumble-down shed at night, and the boys would graze them on a lead rope several times a day.

They set to work cleaning the clutter from the inside of the shed until there was enough room to tie the horses inside for the night. Then they filled their water buckets from the tap outside the house and carried it to the horses. "Well at least we got running water here," Randy commented, remembering the ancient outdoor pump that had been their water source in South Dakota.

"Yeah," replied Carl Jr. "It's gonna be better here, just wait and see!"

Randy looked at his eldest brother for a few long moments. Carl Jr. was starting to show signs of the handsome young man he would soon become, but his fast-growing body was having trouble synchronizing the proportions of its various body parts. He was extra tall with a wiry strength and a physical toughness, due in large part to the harsh years he had endured on the reservation farm.

At this point, his hands and feet seemed to be growing faster than their supporting limbs, making him look gangly and rather awkward. He also was fighting a prolonged battle with pimples, which was frustrating him to no end. He was beginning to take a keen interest in girls, most of whom did not have pimples on their list of desirable attributes in their search for Mr. Right!

They finished tending to the horses for the night, then assisted Charlotte and her junior crew getting the house in order. By nightfall, everything had been carried in and the beds were made up. After a satisfying supper, they headed for bed.

# BATS IN THE BEDROOM

The boys ascended the wide and creaky wooden stairs to the big second story. Michael thought it was awfully spooky, but since he shared a big iron bed with Randy and Randy seemed to be enjoying himself, he swallowed his fears and crawled in. He had just drifted off to sleep when he was jerked awake by a yell from Carl Jr.

"Hey, there's a bird in here," Carl Jr. shouted.

Sure enough, something was flying around in the bedroom. But it was a strange kind of bird, small and black, and it was making a weird staccato clacking noise.

Carl ascended the stairs broom in hand to deal with the intruder. After a spirited chase around the room, he managed to trap the creature. Michael stared at it somewhat horrified. It looked like a very small rat with huge black wings. It sat trapped by the broom and seemed to glare malevolently at them, making its hideous clacking noise through vicious little sharp teeth! Carl killed the creature and threw it out the window, then explained that it was in fact a bat and bats were blind and sort of used their hearing to get around.

With the intruder evicted, they returned to their beds to finish their night's rest. They were blissfully ignorant of the fact that the attic above their heads was infested with bats and despite Carl's best and often creative efforts to evict them, there would be many repeats of that night's bat invasion. In the years to come they would always refer to that house as "The Bat House."

Michael blinked awake the next morning to a brilliant sunrise. Whatever the new human occupants may have thought of the big spooky house, the birds outside obviously had their own opinions and were singing happily in their tweets and chirps. Michael crawled out of bed, navigated around the still unpacked boxes on the floor, and made his way down the big creaky stairway. Charlotte and Carl were sitting in the living room drinking coffee and visiting. Their morning coffee time together was a tradition they followed very seriously. Regardless of their location or circumstances, if they were at the same location, they would sit together and sip their coffee for at least a half hour every morning.

"When are you going to start work for Laverne?" Charlotte was asking her husband. Michael's mind flashed on his handsome uncle Laverne who was married to their favorite aunt Olivia. He didn't know a lot about him but knew he had a small carpentry business and worked mostly around the nearby town of Smithville.

Located on the banks of the mighty Flambeau river, Smithville had an interesting history. The town had grown up on two major industries, logging and farming. In 1840, almost the whole county was covered with six million acres of white pine and hemlock, and loggers made their livings harvesting these trees. The mouth of the Flambeau River lies near Smithville and was an ideal spot from which to float logs down to mills that would saw them into lumber.

The logging industry had fallen off sharply after 1915 and farming then rose to take its place. After all the trees had been cut, farmers would burn the pine stumps to the ground before clearing it. Older residents recalled seeing the stumps burning at night like great torches all over the fields.

Charlotte's father, Joseph Reynolds, had brought his family to this area as a young man, full of talent, strength, and energy. He had carved out a life for his family as a mill hand, logger, and ending up a furniture maker. Although he was descended from an enormously wealthy and entrepreneurial family, the gift of accumulating wealth had totally passed him by. It would also evade most of his descendants, but his intellect and "giftedness" would pass on through his posterity so powerfully that it even seemed to offset the mingling of what might be considered less articulate and gifted bloodlines.

Grandpa Reynolds had pressured Carl and Charlotte to move to a remote farming community downstate instead of moving to this more developed area, but after several trips to scout the area, they had made one of the best decisions ever for their family. Their whole married life had been spent in a desperately poor, mission-orientated rural wooded wasteland, and it was time for civilization. They now were debt free with three thousand, six hundred dollars in the bank from the sale of their farm (minus the cost of the Dodge pickup sporting the sickly excuse of a rack). They would build their future on that.

With the decision made to move to this area, the next big question was which of the two Mennonite churches in the area to attend. The boys wanted to attend the Clayton church where many of their cousins" families attended; but for reasons that were never really clear, Carl and Charlotte decided to join the Glendale church where Charlotte's sister, the popular aunt Olivia and her husband Laverne and their two children, son Henry and daughter Jeanie, were members. This would turn out to be an incredibly good decision for the children.

# NORTH TO ALASKA

Michael's attention was snapped back to the conversation in the living room by his father's next words. "Well," he said, "I thought we might as well do the Alaska trip right away before I get started and while the truck is still in good shape."

*Alaska trip?* Michael marveled, *they are actually planning to do that?* He had heard them talk about taking a road trip to Alaska while they still had some money, but it had seemed like a far-fetched dream that would never happen. Now it seemed like they were serious.

"I want to find a topper for the pickup bed and I'll build a bed across the front for you and me and we will buy a tent for the boys to sleep in. Then I will build a flat plywood box and mount it above the pickup cab to carry supplies."

"What about your sister Leona?" Charlotte asked. "She wants to go along pretty bad, and she could help with the boys."

"Yeah, I thought about that," Carl said. "She can sleep on the floor of the truck bed."

*Wow!* Michael thought, *we are really gonna do this!*

The following weeks were a constant flurry of activity, repairing the tumbledown shed for the horses and stringing electric fences, cleaning the house and finishing the unpacking, and making plans for the big trip. Carl built a large flat plywood box with a lid and mounted it above the cab of the pickup. He decided to paint it to keep it from warping and found a bargain on some paint. The fact that it was a weird shade of gold and matched absolutely nothing seemed not to matter to him. The fact that literally hundreds of fellow motorists would gawk at the ugly creation all the way to Alaska and back was equally unimportant. He had saved a few cents on paint!

As a final touch, Carl built two benches over the wheel wells with storage compartments under them.

The truck was ready to go. Charlotte had spent many hours with Rand McNally road maps spread out on the kitchen table, planning the route and looking for campgrounds and interesting tourist locations, etc. She had put together a very interesting itinerary, which rather than taking the long tedious gravel Alaskan highway, they would head up the west side of Canada through British Columbia then ferry the truck across from the British Columbia coast to the island of Ketchikan Alaska. On the way home, they would tour the great northern States of Montana Wyoming and North Dakota where Carl had relatives still living and farming. Some of them even had ranches which mightily intrigued the horse-crazy Michael. By now, the family excitement was riding high, and they were all eager to head out.

And Leona had arrived, and they planned to head out early the following morning. It was decided the boys could spend the night sleeping in the pickup topper, which would make it easier for them to be ready to leave in the morning. That idea seemed fairly sound, but five rowdy boys trying to sleep in a five foot by eight-foot area had its downsides. Somewhere in the tumbling and shuffling of the night, Carl junior's oversized foot went crashing through the topper window, and they were not able to leave for a few hours until they could get the window fixed.

It was early afternoon by the time the broken window was replaced, and they headed north on the great adventure. The boys had no idea what to expect. Theirs had been a relatively small world, and the longest trips they had experienced were to Ohio and back. They drove until the lengthening shadows announced the coming twilight then checked in at a campground for the night.

Charlotte had done her homework and planned out most of the available camping sites along their route. The new tent was unpacked with gusto, and the boys required little help from Carl to get it set up. It was a sturdy, dome-topped, six-sleeper, and proved to be a good choice. They were soon clustered around a crackling campfire, roasting hot dogs on sharpened sticks. The natural beauty around them was somewhat lost on the Raptor boys since they had been surrounded by it all their lives. However, they did notice the neat, manmade touches like the mowed grass, graded trails, and log edging around campsites. The first night of sleep in the new arrangement went well, and Michael woke rested to the aroma of fresh coffee. His brothers were still sleeping around him, so he threaded his way out of the tent and stepped out in time to see his father pour two cups of coffee from the tin pot gurgling over the fire and hand one to his wife who was emerging drowsily from the pickup camper.

By the time Carl and Charlotte had finished their morning coffee, the boys and Aunt Leona were stirring, and the women began preparing breakfast with Carl in charge of the grill over the fire. Carl was a man who had worked constantly and very hard all his life from his youth into adulthood with very few breaks or vacations. The lackadaisical life of a vacationer would take some adjustment for him, but he would adapt. There would be things that would anger him on the trip, but not once would he give in to his fits of violent rage. It would be many years later when Michael finally figured out that it was likely due in large part to the constant presence of his sister in the family.

They gradually settled into a low-key daily humdrum as the blue Dodge wound its way north and west. The scenery as they wound through the wooded mountains of British Columbia was breathtaking with its white-capped mountain peaks, millions of acres of beautiful timber, and abundant wildflowers on both sides of the roads. The lakes and streams were crystal clear, and the boys gazed down at the swimming fish, which seemed to be just below the surface but were actually many feet below the surface. Often Carl would pull the truck over on the shoulder of the highway, and they would watch the wildlife on and along the road. They watched as enormous Moose and Elk grazed and pushed each other around with their huge antlers. Deer were as plentiful as the small game such as rabbits, coon, foxes, and some species they couldn't positively identify. They especially enjoyed the bears when the mothers would graze as their playful cubs cavorted and tumbled in the thick, lush grass.

# Aunt Olivia and Goat Mountain

Late one evening, they turned into a winding lane which led up to a house in the woods. Charlotte climbed out of the truck and mounted the wooden steps to knock on the door. The door was opened by a strong-looking young man who was married to Charlotte's niece, Carol. He was a friendly guy named Galen, and he welcomed the Raptors in where Carol had a big supper prepared. This night the tent would not need to be pitched, since beds were provided for everyone.

Michael slept well, appreciating the soft mattress in place of the hard ground. When he woke, the sun was streaming in the window. He lay on the bed just being lazy until he heard the crunch of tires coming up the gravel driveway. Curious, he hopped out of bed and peered out the window of the upstairs bedroom. A familiar-looking car was approaching the house. The car stopped near the front porch and Michael smiled as Aunt Olivia and her family emerged. They were also travelling to Alaska but taking a slightly different route. The two families had picked several rendezvous points along the way. Then the plan was to travel over together on the ferry to the island of Ketchikan.

After a huge breakfast, Galen pulled a big flatbed truck up to the porch and invited everyone aboard for a scenic trip up Goat Mountain. The men and children climbed on the back of the truck as the older women squeezed into the cab with Galen. A view became more beautiful as they climbed higher and the trail got narrower until it became a two-track with multiple switchbacks. The switchbacks were places on the trail where the mountainside was too steep to continue carving a trail, so the engineers would make a hairpin turn and continue carving the trail around the other direction until that got too steep and they would carve in another switchback and reverse direction again. The sheer drop at the outer edge of the trail was fearsome, and Aunt Olivia took one look over and froze! "Stop the truck," she croaked as the next switchback loomed ahead! She crawled out of the cab and walked behind until they were through the switchback, then she reclaimed her seat in the truck. She repeated this procedure all the way up and down the mountain. It slowed the tour's progress immensely, but after seeing the terror on her face, no one minded. Michael looked around the truck bed and saw fear on most of the faces with the exception of Carl Jr. He always seemed to enjoy life on the edge. Scary as it was, most of them were having a great time!

When they finally reached the summit, they stopped to enjoy the breathtaking beauty of a British Columbia mountaintop. The trip down was even scarier than the trip up, and Aunt Olivia did a serious amount of walking. By the time they arrived back at the house, Michael was ravenous, and his body felt like it had been dragged behind a galloping horse. The ladies soon had a delicious supper waiting for them, after which the boys were sent to bed early in anticipation of heading out the next morning.

# KETCHIKAN

The next day found them winding their way northwest again, driving through forests alive with wildlife, across rivers and streams, and through huge fields bearing various crops. They were getting closer to the city of Prince Rupert where they would board the ferry to the island of Ketchikan, Alaska. Ketchikan had no highway access, so all traffic there was from the air or sea. The Prince Rupert ferry was one of the closest access by sea but still required a voyage of approximately six hours. Michael was spellbound as he watched the huge ferry boat plowing through the water as it approached the dock. There was a very loud and deep bellow from its foghorn announcing its arrival as it nudged up to the shore. Then an enormous gangplank was slowly extended until the boat was connected to the shore. Soon cars, pickups, and motorcycles were streaming off the ferry as well as a line of pedestrians carrying their handbags, briefcases, and assorted luggage.

When all the incoming vehicles were clear, the barricade for outbound vehicles lifted, and the bumper-to-bumper line of vehicles began to move onto the ferry's huge flat deck. Occupants were required to exit vehicles and take what they would need for the ferry trip with them because the vehicles were packed together too tightly for people to access them.

The hospitality area of the ferry included lounges, a restaurant, and a jukebox. It was the first time Michael had ever seen a jukebox, and he was fascinated by it. He kept feeding it nickels to play the same song over and over, until some of his fellow passengers began to show signs of irritation. Given their upbringing, the Raptor boys had never developed any class or good taste. They were still trying to get past the humiliation of wearing threadbare corduroy trousers when everyone else was wearing blue jeans! For them, life was a slog where you learn as you go—usually the hard or embarrassing way!

Finally, Michael retreated to a secluded spot in the lounge to play with his pocketknife collection. He had been buying different and unusual knives at the various tourist stops for souvenirs from the trip, and he had several rather unique ones and some with beautiful pictures painted on the handles.

When the deep foghorn of the ferry announced their approach to the Ketchikan dock, passengers lined up at the rail to watch the docking procedure. Then those with vehicles had to make their way to the exiting vehicles where they climbed in and rode ashore.

Ketchikan was wooded and very mountainous. Carl and Charlotte had decided to pay the extra cost of bringing their vehicle across because it served as their sleeping quarters. By now, the family was a well-oiled machine when it came to setting up at a campsite. Michael was not known for his energetic cooperation when there was work to be done, so usually Carl Jr. and Randy went ahead with the tent setup and sent him out to gather wood. He would amble around rather aimlessly and admire the scenery and check out other people's camping equipment from the surrounding woods. He had fine-tuned a sound effect performance which he called "man coming down with the flu." It started with a few watery-sounding gags then progressed into an awful moan with choking heaves, culminating with the unmistakable gurgly sound of stomach contents gushing out to the ground. He knew it was a very good act, but it disgusted and revolted absolutely everyone who heard it. It was most effective just outside the campfire light when hungry people gathered around picnic tables were just beginning to dig into the roasted hot dogs and potato salad. The sound effect caused voracious appetites to disappear in the blink of an eye! He was careful not to get caught, but who could criticize a poor sick person losing their stomach contents out in the brush?

Once when he was wandering around the campground, Michael caught the eye of a chatty elderly gentleman who engaged him in conversation. The man had asked the usual questions such as "where are you from, where are you headed, and how long to you plan to be gone," etc. Michael answered the questions with the best of his rather limited knowledge, then the man asked, "And how did you find the roads?"

Michael stared at him for a long moment then said, "Well, we have maps and stuff!" For some reason, he couldn't figure out, this answer seemed to amuse the old gentleman. Unfortunately for him, the conversation was overheard by Aunt Leona who had a great time relating it to the family around the campfire that evening. Everyone seemed to think it was a very funny story—except Michael! After all, they *did* have maps and that *was* how they found which roads to take!

The next day, they visited a pulp logging mill built into the side of a hill near the sea. A tour guide showed them every step of the process from the loads of raw logs that rumbled in on the huge logging trucks, through the process of floating them into the mill via huge, water-filled concrete canals to where the bark was peeled off with jets of extremely high pressure water. Then the logs were cut up and pulverized for the making of paper pulp. The raw power and brute force employed in the entire operation was awe-inspiring. The water pressure, they were informed, could cut a man's arm off in seconds.

On the way back to their campsite that afternoon, Carl spotted an old wrecked car in the woods beside the road which had obviously been there for months if not years. When the family was setting up camp that evening and preparing supper, he returned and retrieved the Alaska license plate from the wreck for his trip souvenir. Michael was rather surprised that he had taken something that wasn't his, but he decided on further reflection that since it was scrap it wasn't much different than taking a rock or some form of plant life.

# COWBOYS AND BUGGY SAILS

They returned to the mainland on the ferry where Michael again kept the marvelous jukebox busy playing his song, "Green Green" by a group called the New Christy Minstrels.

The trip home was much more interesting to him than the trip up. They stopped at one of Carl's Montana ranch relatives where they raised cattle and worked them with horses. They also had farm equipment for making hay and raising some small grain crops such as wheat, oats, and barley. The most fascinating thing on this ranch though was an ancient restored automobile. There was no starter or even an engine crank. The engine was started by raising one of the drive wheels and spinning it until the engine roared to life. This was the same starting system the Raptor boys had used on many of their homemade go-carts, which made them feel rather competent. They might have a future in mechanical engineering yet! The rancher took them for a dusty ride around the ranch in the old car then parked it carefully back in the shed.

The next day found them back in the truck headed south and east again. They stopped at a rest stop and were relaxing and admiring the scenery when a rider-less horse galloped up to the fence across the road and stopped. The horse was wearing a saddle and bridle, but the reins to the bridle were dragging on the ground.

Carl immediately crawled through the fence to try to catch the agitated animal. He managed to catch it, then he swung up into the saddle. He would later claim he was going to look for the missing rider, but Michael was pretty sure he just couldn't resist riding the horse! It turned out to be an exceedingly short ride! He was hardly more than in the saddle when a cowboy emerged from the trees. He was furious with Carl for taking liberties with his horse and let him know it. Carl's excuses sounded weak and lame, and the boys were awestruck at seeing their great and mighty father get a verbal beat-down. It was the only time they would ever witness such a thing, and they found it a bit shocking.

Their last stop to visit relatives was on the endless empty plains of North Dakota. The boys gaped at the enormous farm equipment used on these huge dryland farms. There were rows of scraggly little trees which had been planted along the roads and at strategic places for windbreakers and erosion barriers. The ubiquitous howling wind blew dirt and topsoil around, at times so densely it was difficult to see.

Carl told a story from his childhood how a young couple had taken a horse and buggy out into the country for a picnic. They had unhitched the horse and tied it to the buggy while they were picnicking, but something spooked it badly, and it jerked loose and raced for home.

Stranded with a useless buggy and facing a very long walk home, the young man got creative and fashioned the buggy shafts and picnic blanket into a makeshift sail, which powered them back home. Seeing and feeling the power of the wind around them, the boys had no trouble believing the story!

The next day, they piled their bags and bodies in the truck and headed for Mt. Rushmore, South Dakota. The boys were duly impressed by the clear and unmistakable faces of the former presidents carved high up in the rocky bluff. From there, they drove into the badlands where the boys had a great time running across the rough terrain and along knife-edge ridges. Their parents gave them plenty of time to run off their pent-up energy.

Night was coming on fast by the time the truck rumbled back on the paved highway. They hadn't been able to locate a campground, so they scanned the countryside as they drove for a place to pitch camp. Finally, in desperation, Carl turned into a two-track dirt lane back into a field to a scraggly stand of trees. They had just pitched the tent and were starting to prepare supper when they heard the distant roar of a truck headed their way. Through the gathering dusk, they could see a ranch tuck roaring their way at a high rate of speed. The truck appeared to be off-road, and it was kicking up a huge dust cloud making it appear as if the truck was trying to outrun an approaching tornado.

"Quick!" Carl shouted, grabbing the tent and collapsing the support poles. "Shove this tent in the truck bed and let's get out of here!"

There was a mad scramble as they collapsed the tent enough to stuff it in the back of the pickup, then everyone scrambled into the truck, and Carl jammed the truck in gear and they raced back toward the main road with the slant six engine screaming. It would be many years later when Michael lived in Wyoming that he would realize the gravity of what they had done. These ranchers may own and control thousands of acres of land, but every square inch of it is as sacred to them as the living room in their houses. Most of them carry rifles in their trucks, and many of them still carry holstered pistols.

It was very late before they found a pull-off along the road where they re-pitched the tent and spent the rest of the night. No one enjoyed a restful night's sleep after the drama.

Morning found a tired and subdued group of campers. The trip was beginning to wear them down, and most of them were ready to get back home to normal living. Michael was missing the horses and wondering if they were okay. None of them were sure what the new life in Ohio would bring, but it was time to start living it. They travelled long days, stopping only for food and fuel, and finally found themselves turning in the driveway to the huge old dilapidated house.

The next day, Carl Jr. and Randy were helping Charlotte unpack the camping gear and supplies from the truck while Carl ordered Michael to help him make some more repairs to the horse shed. There were still gaping holes in some of the walls, and Carl was salvaging planks to reinforce them. He instructed Michael to hold the planks in place while he drove the nails. But Michael was having a hard time understanding what he wanted because there seemed to be no rhyme or reason to how his father was attempting to effect the repairs. He was becoming more nervous and fearful as he sensed the anger growing in his father, and finally he made the egregious error of not holding a board at the proper angle.

*"Hold that board, you fat ba——d!"* his father roared. Michael cringed inside. He was used to being belittled and accused of being fat to the point where he thought of himself as fat. Indeed, he tended to be a bit on the chubby side at times, but his brothers were stick thin, making him look heavy by comparison. It made him angry when his brothers mocked him and hurt deeply when his parents mocked him, but now he was a "fat ba——d." That was a new low! *What does my father know about my conception that I don't?* he thought bitterly!

Sunday morning found the family scrubbed and in their Sunday best, headed for their new church. The Glendale Mennonite church was much larger than the reservation chapel had been, and its people were totally friendly. There were children and young people there all of their ages, and there was a small but active youth group. The youth group included kids as young as thirteen, so Michael found himself invited to youth activities. But where some of the other thirteen-year-olds fit in reasonably well, Michael was having trouble knowing how to act properly. For the first time in his life, he was beginning to understand that he was actually a person. Having grown up more like property than persons, all their decisions had been made for them, and all attempts at self-expression brutally beat into submission. But that had been on an isolated Indian reservation where adults could do what they pleased and were accountable to no one. This was a whole different social situation.

# CHURCH DIVISION

The Glendale church was a white frame building located about a half-hour drive from the Raptors' new home. The church had only one leader, Pastor Lowell. They had been through serious problems years before which had led to division and two Mennonite churches in the area. Pastor Lowell was now a bit leery of working with other pastors, and he did a fine job of shepherding his congregation with the assistance of some very fine men in the group. The Raptor boys began to look forward to Sunday church services for more than just social reasons. Pastor Lowell was not a spellbinding orator, but he did have interesting things to say in his sermons. His preaching style was conversational rather than the high and lofty drone of most preachers of the day. Carl and Charlotte with their boys were welcomed into the congregation with open arms and friendly smiles. Their congregation freely shared their victories and struggles in life with each other. In time, Carl was voted in as the superintendent of the Sunday school.

The older Raptor boys, however, were somewhat more interested in the "very fine girls" in the group, and there was a fair supply of them. Pastor Lowell Miller had two daughters, Bertha, the eldest, and Rene who was a couple years younger. They were outgoing, intelligent, and just plain fun! There were also two brothers named John and Isaac Kurtz who had fairly large and talented families.

The Raptor boys were surprised at how the adults treated them with respect and took genuine interest in them. John had a son named Donnie who was about Michael's age, and they became friends. Donnie and Michael never became super tight friends, but they would spend a lot of time together, and Michael came to depend on Donnie, who taught him a multitude of social and everyday life things that he had never learned.

And it was Donnie who on a warm, lazy Sunday afternoon, would totally blow his mind by thoroughly but not crudely explaining the "facts of life" to him, including the physiological differences between boys and girls. Donnie had gone into great detail and left Michael's head spinning as he contemplated it all. But the one thing Donnie had not explained, due to his lack of experience, was the associated pleasure, lust, and devastation it could all bring to the human race.

There was another family named Stevens who was prominent in the Glendale church. The father, Mike, was a tall, tough-looking man who had a wicked sense of humor and seemed to be admired by most of the men and all of the women, although not in an inappropriate way. He was a hard-working farmer who seemed to love his work and his family. His eldest son, Clayton, was about Carl Jr.'s age, and they became friends. He had a younger son named Leighton who was closer to Randy's age and they became very close friends. Leighton had an intense personality and pursued everything he did with passion and determination. His adventurous nature would lead him into many interesting situations.

The selection of the fairer sex was a dynamic of significantly more interest to Carl Jr. than to his siblings at this point. He had taken a fairly keen interest in one of the pastor's daughters back in the reservation chapel, but for some murky, unexplained reason, their parents had done their best to make sure their sons did not get involved with the pastor's daughters. Many years later when a skeleton finally tumbled from the family closet, he would discover that she was his cousin. There was no ensuing crisis however because the Raptor home was a dictatorship, and the family had only one provision in their "Bill of Rights"—the right to remain silent! Carl and Charlotte had a deeply held and closely guarded secret which created this necessity, and no explanation was even considered. It would be years before the secret would grudgingly be revealed.

The Glendale youth group was an active and diverse group of young people with several of the older ones providing energy and momentum. Perhaps the most prominent among them was the high-voltage cousin Henry. His younger sister Jeanie was also active and fun. For some reason, it seemed that Cousin Henry had decided to make a project out of civilizing his backward cousins. He went out of his way to include them in all social activities. He even included thirteen-year-old Michael, whose many embarrassing social gaffes and inappropriate remarks would have made a redneck cringe! He was also the least athletic of the older brothers who were not themselves athletic at all. They had played some backyard softball growing up, and there were occasional softball games at church functions, but Michael had begun to avoid them after something he had said or done had angered his big tough adopted half-Indian uncle Rusty who took his revenge by "accidentally" smashing a fastball into the side of Michael's head. Those who saw it happen knew it was not an accident, but no one had the courage to speak up against uncle Rusty, so there were no repercussions for him.

# ALL SPORTS OF MUSIC

With time, their sports skills began to improve, especially Carl Jr. and Randy's, who were tough from their reservation farm life. Michael preferred the inside group games they played, and his inherited wit and humor helped overshadow some of his gaffes. One of his favorite games was called the Prince of Paris a game with a high-pressure caller requiring instant response before he called you out, and you would have to move to the back of the line. The idea was to work your way to the head position in line and then defend it while others tried to throw you out via quicker responses. Henry was the hands down best caller and very good at knocking people back to the end of the line.

Another thing that united this youth group was their love of music. Most of the group were good singers, and the Isaac Kurtz kids were incredibly gifted on instruments, especially guitars. Isaac himself played guitar, and some of his sons took guitar playing to a whole new level.

In the earlier days, the eldest son, Leon was the main attraction. He could bring a guitar to life like no one Michael had ever known. He was a popular, average-looking guy with an average build, but he was always popular with his sense of humor and fun-loving ways. Michael was somewhat in awe of him at first but eventually came to see him as one of the older guys in the group who many admired. Eventually his younger brother grew up and displayed equal or greater guitar playing ability.

The Kurtz family also sang together, and the whole congregation thoroughly enjoyed their special music. The older Raptor boys had inherited musical ability from their mother, especially Michael who had an ear for rhythm and harmony. He and Randy had often sung duets for the little mission church back in South Dakota. But there was very little singing in their home. Somehow singing was uncool and inappropriate in their family setting.

But now there was a whole new outlet for music outside the strictures of their family, and Michael ate it up! He wanted to play guitar so badly he could almost taste it, but the harder he tried to master the cheap guitar his parents had given him for Christmas, the more frustrated he got. He bought several how-to books, but each of them had a different approach, and all of them were confusing. Once, they had another family over for supper who convinced him to bring out the guitar and show them what he had learned so far. He showed them the pitifully few things he had learned so far, then Charlotte grabbed the guitar and said, "It's really not that hard!" as she dramatically banged on the strings and swayed to mock a professional singer. As she banged and swayed, her tongue was extended and licking her lips in an exaggerated mockery. Everyone present knew that Michael had always struggled with chapped lips, which she blamed on him for licking them. Her mockery fell flat, but Michael was pretty sure she didn't mind because it had been a perfect way to demean and belittle him. His face was deep red as he slunk from the room. He had to be content to sing along as the Kurtz kids worked their magic on the strings.

Once, a very skilled guitarist from another state came to their home to visit, and Michael talked him into playing his guitar. The young man managed to squeeze some music out of it, but he very tactfully told Michael that the guitar was almost too cheap to make music. Meanwhile the desire to learn to play continued to burn and grow within his soul. Little did he know that God would one day bring an unlikely young man into his world who would bring the dream to life!

# SUMMER AND SHARING

Summer was passing rapidly, with the specter of a new school becoming ever larger. Michael tried not to think of school as they thought up ways to amuse themselves. They spent much time on the banks of the mighty Flambeau river trying to create functional rafts with severely limited success. Eventually they came to realize that life was far less complex if they just aired up some old inner tubes and floated on them instead of hacking around on semirotted "logs" and tying them together with the always-available baler twine.

Another sporting event was towing the little red Radio Flyer wagon on a long rope behind the horses. With only two horses serving the four older boys, they needed to leverage the equine contribution. They saddled Dusty and tied a forty-foot-long rope to the saddle horn with the other end secured to the handle of the little red wagon. They thought little Johnny would be a good candidate, so he was first up in the wagon. As the horse's speed increased from a trot to a canter, then a full gallop, they discovered a flaw in their entertainment package. The wagon bounced so hard over the ruts in the field that Johnny was bouncing so hard that several times he was very nearly thrown from the wagon. Michael and Randy held a quick consultation about this problem then hurried into the house and retrieved several trouser belts which they strung under the wagon and across his lap. They had just begun to rejoice in the success of this plan when one of their uncles drove up the lane. He took one look at their setup and grounded them immediately, pending a consultation with their mother. Charlotte was horrified and ordered them to put the horse and wagon away and never try a stunt like that again. The sting of her rebuke was somewhat mitigated by the total success of their efforts!

Carl had begun his job working for Uncle Laverne. He soon discovered that while his brother-in-law could be socially entertaining, he had another side which came out at work. He could be irritable and short-tempered and make nasty comments when he was upset. Carl, who was used to taking orders from his former boss, the kind and grandfatherly Pastor Randy, had trouble getting used to this new work life. Carl was gifted at cobbling materials together to make anything he needed, but when it came to carpentry and craftsmanship, customers wanted things done well and properly. But the bills needed paid, and he needed to work somewhere, so he tried to follow orders and do what was required of him. He would never really know the fulfilment that two of his sons would one day know—that of building strong, well-designed structures that were pleasing to the eye.

The years of work in Rango, however, were beginning to take a toll on Carl's health. He and his father had travelled to Rango back in South Dakota for weeks at a time to work for Pastor Randy who had masonry contracts there. They had rented a damp basement room to sleep in at night, and Carl had developed arthritis. Each year that passed made it worse, and he lived on pain medications and at times even walked with a cane. Doctors and chiropractors were of little assistance for his condition. He was, however, as good at handling physical pain as he was handing it out. He rarely complained or even mentioned it.

At one time, the pain got so severe he was not able to work for several weeks. The church people were concerned and offered to come over and assist them with anything they need help with, but Charlotte assured them that her and her big strong boys were well able to handle things on their own. Carl even missed church services which was nearly unheard of.

One Sunday morning when he was not present, the current Sunday school superintendent announced that this being a fifth Sunday offering, the proceeds were not designated yet, and he would like to suggest that it be given to the Raptors who had been without income for several weeks. There was a murmur of enthusiastic agreement across the congregation, but the superintendent said, "I don't think Charlotte agrees!"

Michael looked across at his mother and saw that her face had a slight flush, and she was shaking her head vigorously from side to side. The chapel fell silent, and Michael saw the phony smile on her face that she always used for visiting preachers or someone she wanted to impress. "No thanks," she said, her voice tight with emotion. "We're doing just fine!"

Michael's gaze swept the congregation, and he saw disappointment on many faces. They all knew the Raptors were not going to lose their house or die of starvation, but they wanted to help make their lives a little bit better. What they didn't know was that the Raptors were existing on Carl's unemployment checks which amounted to slightly over fifty dollars per week. It was just more than Charlotte's pride could handle, and Michael felt a wave of irritation. *Why did his folks work so hard to pretend they were the perfect family with no needs?*

Many years later when he was himself a missionary, a retired missionary gave him some advice he never forgot. Michael was trying to refuse a gift, and the old gentleman said, "Let me pass on to you what I was told by an older missionary. Sometimes it takes more grace to receive than it does to give. You should not deny someone the pleasure of sharing with you!"

# SCHOOL DAZE

The day, Michael dreaded finally arrived. It was time to register for school. Charlotte loaded the boys into the old Chevy, and they drove into the heart of Smithville, a town of just over 3,600 people. They parked in the big paved parking lot beside the big brick school building. They climbed the long, steep concrete steps to the main entrance, and once inside, the boys were directed to the various locations where student enrollment corresponded with their ages and grades. Michael found himself alone in a large hall where a table and several chairs were set up rather haphazardly. A medium-sized and rather compactly built middle-aged man was manning the desk, but he was constantly coming and going. Michael would later learn that he was the school principal, and he obviously had more irons in his proverbial fire today than he could efficiently juggle. In a deep, gravelly voice, he instructed Michael to have a seat and wait for him to return. The problem was the table and chairs were set up in such a way that Michael couldn't tell which side of the table to sit on so he just chose a side and sat down. Had he not been so totally nervous, he might have gathered a few clues such as which side had the registration forms and which side the official paperwork and pile of completed applications. Another more perceptive person might have assumed that the side toward the entrance door would logically be for students! He managed to choose the wrong side.

The longer he sat in the comfortable padded swiveling office chair, the more nervous he became. Finally, he decided to pass the time by perusing the piles of paperwork on the desk. He was busily fingering through said papers when Principal Breckman returned. His interview began with a stinging rebuke and rather clear explanation of on which side of the table he belonged! There were also clear instructions set forth concerning the impropriety of him perusing the documents on the table which were "none of his business!" It was an ignoble beginning to the rest of his less than impressive academic life. He never told anyone of this utterly humiliating beginning.

On the first day of school, all the students were lined up in the main hall then divided by grades and assigned "homerooms." Michael felt the curious stares of the other students on him. New students were few in this little farming town, and that made the Raptor boys objects of curiosity. He was rather socially challenged, and his brothers also needed to up their social acumen. In the reservation schools, they had tasted a bit of minority treatment. Michael was also struggling with the new dynamics of being viewed as a person.

In the closed and very private setting in which they had been raised, the Raptor children had been regarded and treated as property. Somewhere in the back of their parents' minds, there was probably a fuzzy concept that they were raising future people, but in the Raptor home, all decision making whether large or small was made by the parents. This included everything from hairstyles (ridiculous home administered butch jobs) to clothing (if it's close to your size you're gonna wear it) and including scheduling, and daily behavior right down to how much toilet paper you were allowed (three squares of tissue per episode were sufficient per Charlotte's dictate). Michael was never quite sure if she was serious about that rule and would supplement the three squares with pages from the Sears and Roebuck catalog, torn out and crumpled multiple times to make them semi-absorbent.

Now here in this new school environment, they were actually given choices! They could select classes, friends, what to do during lunch hour, etc. This was a breath of fresh air to Carl. Jr. who had never seemed to have any doubt that he was a person too and fully capable of making at least some of his own decisions. This tended to make him the tip of the emancipation spear since as the oldest child, he was always breaking new ground. Carl and Charlotte struggled to maintain their dictatorial stranglehold on the children, but ever so gradually, their iron grip began to slip.

Another huge change for the boys was riding the school bus. The old normal had them riding in the clunkiest school bus in the fleet, prone to breakdowns in the middle of nowhere on cold winter days and driven by a half breed who was often so drunk at the wheel that his speech was badly slurred and made no sense. Many times, the bus was freezing cold, and the windows frosted completely over. Their route had the worst record in the whole school for tardiness. Some days, the bus wouldn't show up at all if the driver called in sick (drunk). On occasion, the students would find beer stashed under the seats.

In their new world, they were picked up in a big beautiful clean bus with good heaters and a cheery fun-loving driver named Rick. Rick kept telling the Raptor boys to be real careful on the Flambeau. His voice would become husky, and his face would take on a mock scared, conspiratorial look as his quivering voice warned them to beware the hungry alligators lurking just below the surface of the water! The boys would laugh off his warnings, but Michael was mighty cautious when playing in the river. It didn't help that his brothers confidently assured him that the gators would naturally eat him first given his extra body fat.

The boys adapted fairly well in the new school. Carl Jr.'s grades were very good, and Randy's were outstanding, much to his mother's delight. Michael's grades were…passable. He found school studies boring and spent most of his time reading books about horses and cowboys.

Every morning recess, milk was supplied at no charge for all students. The milk came in large plastic bags with white rubber hoses about one half inch in diameter and six inches long. A big stain-less-steel dispensing machine stood in the hallway, and the bags were inserted in the tops of it with the rubber hose sticking out through a shutoff valve. Students were issued paper cups and would stand in line while the designated teacher filled their cups with the deliciously cold white liquid.

For some reason, the white rubber hoses were highly prized by students, and when the milk bags were empty, they would beg the teacher to cut off the hose and give it to them, which they always did.

The hoses became one of several forms of school currency and were traded for other coveted items of equal or greater worthlessness.

Playground games were not organized by the staff, but students organized their own games. One of Michael's favorite games was the unofficial marble tournaments. Students would bring marbles and take turns trying to roll them into an opponent's marble. If they were successful, they got to keep the opponent's marble. Winners were determined by who had the most and best marbles. Losers were the ones who lost their marbles! Some marbles were larger than others and were more valuable. But the most valuable of all were the highly prized "steelies." They were actually stainless-steel balls from ball bearings and were very hard to come by. They could not be bought in stores, so the supply was limited to what the fortunate boys with mechanic fathers would bring. One medium-sized steelie was worth five or six similar-sized marbles.

The teachers at the Smithville school kept better order than they had been used to at their former school, but it seemed like it was just a job to them. There was no effort to make learning exciting or even interesting. It was like a huge buffet of facts and information, and it was up to the students to absorb them.

On the social scene, the Raptor boys didn't make many friends from school. The twin dynamics of their upbringing and their way out of the mainstream religious life made it difficult for them to interact easily with other students. But they had their friends from church, so they were not friendless.

# TWINKLE AND FLICKA

Church life, however, was a very different story. There were soft-ball games, ice hockey in the winter, and a host of social events. Some of their new friends were very interested in their horses, and it wasn't long until Dusty and Twinkle had more customers than they could handle.

Soon after they moved from the bat house to the farm, Carl decided to have Twinkle, the black mare bred. He located a stallion and got her hauled over to him for servicing, but Twinkle would not accept him.

Two months later, it became obvious that she was already pregnant and would be dropping her foal very soon. Michael was beside himself with excitement, and every morning he woke early and ran out to the pasture to see if the foal had come yet. Finally, one morning he found her with a beautiful little smoke gray filly at her heels. Michael was instantly in love and spent every spare minute with them. Eventually, his father offered to trade his half of the foal for Michael's half of the mare, to which Michael readily agreed. He named her Flicka after a horse in a book he had thoroughly enjoyed. Although he would eventually own dozens of horses and raise many foals, none was ever more special than little Flicka.

Carl solved the horse shortage problem in what Michael considered the best possible way. Back on the reservation, they had been training a pair of sorrel mares for a neighbor who never used them. The mares ran with a stallion who was very serious about his husbandry duty, so the next two years produced two sets of babies.

Unbeknownst to the boys, Carl bought all six horses and colts and had them shipped in. The day the big cattle truck rumbled in the drive and dropped the big ramp to unload, its cargo was one of the happiest days in Michael's young life! There were two mares—two two-year-old fillies, and two one-year-olds. Only the mares had had any training at all, and their training had been pretty basic. The two-year-old ones were ready to begin training, and Michael latched onto a rich dark brown one with flaxen, honey-colored mane and tail. She proved to be fast under a saddle and strong under a harness. Michael and Carl believed that there must have been a strong strain of Morgan in her ancestry.

Sunday afternoon trail rides became common with the arrival of additional mounts. They had six horses they could ride and mounted their church friends on the best trained mounts with the best equipment. A couple of the Raptor boys always had to ride bareback with bridles cobbled together from old harness sets, but Michael didn't mind at all. He loved feeling the powerful horses' muscles work between his knees, and in the winter, the warmth from the horse would rise through their shaggy winter coats to warm his legs.

When the horses were trained to ride and pull, Carl rounded up wagons for them to pull in the summer and sleighs for the winter. He became known for providing the conveyances for horse drawn hay-rides. It was fun to hear the jingle of harness and clip-clop of hooves instead of the roar of a tractor in the crisp night air as they cruised down the road and across the fields.

Carl had brought the old homemade horse cart along when they moved, and that was also part of the entertainment. Carl had cobbled the cart together from the axle of a Model T. It was a very crude contraption with an old bus seat and shafts made of slender Aspen poles hacked directly from the woods. Carl Jr. discovered iron handles sticking inward from the wheels which would activate brakes when twisted. That novelty was short lived though. They wanted speed, not brakes!

# THE SWIMMING HOLE

One day while Carl junior was sitting in math class, the teacher said out of the blue that he has an old Ford Fairlane for sale that needs a flywheel, and he will sell it for $100. Carl Jr. thought that sounded like a good deal so he went home and asked his parents if they would want to buy it, and they suggested that he buy it. He jumped on the opportunity, and soon he was the proud owner of a 1960 Ford Fairlane two-door. It was black and powered by a six-cylinder motor with a three-speed column shifter. He fixed the flywheel but hadn't driven it long until the transmission went out. By now, he was enthused about doing his own mechanical work, so he went to a salvage yard for a used transmission. The guys at the salvage yard suggested that he might want to put his shifter on the floor. He took their suggestion and then went on to accessorize the inside of the car. There was a hole in the dash where some instruments had been removed, so he made a hardwood plaque and inscribed the words "Jump in sardine, here's your tin!" Thus began a new era for the Raptor boys. Carl Jr. had his license and a car, and they were mobile! Of course, with the status quo in the Raptor household, every outing in the car whether large or small required permission from controlling parents. But Carl Jr. was in a quest to spread his wings and experience life a bit more.

Swimming had always been a favorite activity for the boys, and there was a good swimming spot a few miles away. It was a bit too far for biking, but the Fairlane could whisk them there in no time. Occasionally they would take friends along if some were in the area. On one occasion, some longtime family friends from out of state were there visiting, and the boys all piled in for a trip to the swimming hole. They took along some inflated inner tubes for flotation, and this time Johnny got to go along. The older boys regarded him as a bit of a nuisance, especially since he didn't know how to swim, so sometimes he had to stay home.

The swimming hole was just a short stretch of lake shore that tapered gradually into deeper water. Johnny was soon floating happily on one of the inflated inner tubes while the older boys swam and splashed. The oldest of the visiting boys could not swim either, but he waded out and splashed around. After a time, he spied Johnny floating in nearly six-foot-deep water and decided to commandeer his tube. Unaware that Johnny could not swim, he unceremoniously dumped him off the tube into the deep water, and instantly Johnny began flailing and screaming for help.

Carl Jr. was on the shore partially dressed when he heard the commotion. He turned to see what was happening, and his blood ran cold as he literally watched his little brother begin to drown! The visiting boy was the only one close to him, but he was of no help because he couldn't swim himself. Carl Jr. instantly recalled training he had gotten in school about safety and rescue. He knew if he swam out to his brother, there was a very serious risk of his brother pulling them both under. He searched his surroundings desperately until he found a large stick which he grabbed and plunged into the water with it. He was a strong swimmer and managed to reach Johnny who was flailing for his very life. "Johnny, *grab this!*" he shouted as he thrust the end of the stick toward the floundering boy. Johnny grasped the proffered stick, and Carl Jr. towed him to shallower water where he could grab him and carry him to shore.

It was a very sober group of boys that left the swimming hole that night. They agreed that no one would mention it to their parents. That was normal for the Raptor boys; they knew better than to share anything with their parents. The visiting kids also kept it quiet, and Carl Jr.'s heroics would never be acknowledged. But everyone at the swimming hole that evening knew without a doubt that he had saved his little brother's life, and no one else there could have!

# EXCAVATING AND BIRCH TREES

One hard-and-fast rule was absolutely no dating before the age of eighteen which Carl Jr. observed, but it didn"t keep him from interacting with the young ladies in the youth group. When he was finally old enough, he began to ask them out on dates. The Glendale youth group interacted with another Mennonite church about seventy-five miles away named Birchwood Mennonite church. Carl Jr. began to notice an attractive black-haired girl from there named Carol. They dated long enough to become known as a couple. She was a quiet and unassuming young woman which bothered him some. He had had a long-held interest in a young lady from another state who was much more outgoing, but competition for her affections was rather strong. When she broke up with her current boyfriend, she started to come on to Carl. Jr., so he decided to break up with Carol and date her.

For some reason, Michael needed to ride home from the youth function with them the night Carl Jr. gave her the bad news. They stood just outside the car door to talk, and he heard it all. He felt very sorry for Carol who handled it with a mature grace. But the hurt and disappointment in her voice was unmistakable. In one of life's little ironies, the new romance was destined to fizzle and die, but Carol would one day marry the new girl's brother.

Decades later as middle-aged married couples, Michael's family and her family would cross paths and get to know each other well, and he would often think of what a fine woman his big brother walked away from that night.

The biggest event of their first year in Ohio was the purchase of a small tumbledown farm located on the curve of a gravel road several miles north of Smithville. The house was small and in bad condition, and the large barn was literally falling down. It had become obvious that the bat house would not be adequate to survive the winter, so the move was made. Carl immediately began building a sizable addition to the house and hired an excavator named Brian from the Clayton Mennonite church to totally redo the landscaping. He was a robust friendly man who was very good at his job. They took out most to the trees around the house and planted grass.

Several hundred yards north of the old barn, there was a beautiful stand of white birch trees and behind them was a large pond. The big dozer pushed dirt from the yard down around the birch trees a couple feet deep to fill in the swampy area and let grass grow. The finished effect was beautiful the first year, until the birch trees started dying. They learned too late that filling in all that dirt around the base of the trees had effectively smothered the roots. All the beautiful white trees died that next year. Michael would have much preferred that they leave all the trees standing, but his mother had a natural flair for landscaping, and in the end, he realized it had been tastefully done.

Some months later, they were shocked to hear that excavator Brian had been involved in a serious mishap. He had been driving his truck along a county road when some boys began throwing rocks at his truck. One of the rocks shattered the window in his cab, sending sharp shards into his face. One of the shards sliced his eyeball, blinding him permanently in that eye. Later when he had recovered, he went to their house to tell them that he forgave them and held no bitterness toward them, but their mother met him angrily at the door of the house and ordered him to go away and not bother them again or they would sue him!

# SEEDLINGS IN THE SWAMP

Charlotte had always been quick to remove trees in unwanted locations, but she was equally motivated to plant or transplant new trees. This was one lifelong hobby that would be picked up by several of her sons, especially Johnny and Michael. But it would be many years before they would experience the real fulfillment of nourishing them and watching them grow. As a small boy, Michael had been fascinated by "helping" his mother plant several seedling trees as she explained to him that they would grow into large shade trees one day. She had neglected to emphasize the timetable involved though, so when Michael scurried out early the next morning to see how much they had grown, he was sorely disappointed by their lack of progress! He tried giving them more water, but the spindly little things didn't seem grow at all. He went back into the house and reported to his mother that her trees were not growing like she said they would. She had then explained to him that all living things grow at different speeds, and trees take many years to grow.

Now, years later, planting trees and plants was the one thing Michael always enjoyed doing with his mother. Their new property adjoined a huge forest and swamp. The neighbors warned them that the swamp had bottomless bogs that would suck whole animals under to their deaths. But the swamps were teeming with fascinating plant and wildlife, and often Charlotte and Michael would venture deep into them in search of seedlings or plants to dig up and carry home to replant. It was on one of these excursions that Michael's science schooling met real life.

While Michael was for the most part a very unmotivated student, when he came across something that interested him, he poured

49

himself into learning about it. He loved reading books and writing book reports about them, so English was one of the few classes he aced. His English teachers would often read his book reports or other writings as an example to the rest of the class. Occasionally the other subjects would veer into things that would grab his attention but not often enough to hold his attention long enough to score well in the dreadful report card. Recently in science class, they had been studying plant life, and he found that interesting. The most fascinating plant of all had been the carnivorous pitcher plant. The plant was shaped like a pitcher, and the inside of its mouth was lined with red streaks resembling blood veins. Insects would fly or crawl in seeking blood, and the plant would close up and digest them for nourishment. On one of his trips deep into the swamp with his mother, Michael was amazed and overjoyed to discover an actual pitcher plant. He called his mother over and excitedly shared with her what the plant was called and how it worked. It was one of the few times in life that he would actually teach her something! They discussed briefly whether it would be possible to dig it up and transplant it at home, but they both agreed that the plant would probably not survive the transplant, and besides that, there were so many more insects to nourish it here in the heart of the swamp, so they left it alone. In the months and years to come, Michael always looked for another pitcher plant in their swamp excursions, but he never found another one.

The Raptor boys were always looking for more places to ride their horses. The big swamp was off limits for riding though by strict orders from their father. There were no roads through the swamp, and although as a bird flies, the narrowest part was less than a half mile across. It was necessary to drive miles around the swamp to get across to that point. There was a rather unusual straight open path through the swamp at the narrowest point where no trees or large vegetation grew. One day, Carl encountered a grizzled old-timer who told him the story of that strip through the swamp.

Many years before there were roads throughout the county, loggers were cutting the large timber on this side of the swamp. The swamp was between them and the mighty Flambeau river where they hauled their logs to float them down to the mills. They had decided that instead of hauling the logs the many miles around the swamp, they would build what was known as a corduroy road across this narrow neck in the swamp.

They spent weeks creating what basically amounted to a very long raft of logs bound tightly together all the way across the swamp. When the road was finally finished, the teamsters lined up their long caravan of wagons piled high with logs and hauled them across the new road. The road worked great, and they were thrilled with their genius idea and all the weeks and miles it would save them. But as the last wagon load of logs trundled off the new road and up the bank, a horrified shout went up from some of the onlookers. The driver of the last wagon turned to look behind him. He was shocked when he realized that the entire corduroy road was moving. The swamp was sucking it down! Slowly but relentlessly, the bottomless bog sucked the new road down into its murky depths, leaving a group of teamsters shaking in their muddy boots! Apparently, the road was still somewhere under there precluding trees and large vegetation from taking root.

# WINTER WHISTLING

Winters here could be cold and snowy, but since the area was much more prosperous than where they had come from, roads were promptly plowed with large and well-maintained equipment. The Raptors were also informed that if they wished to have the county plows plow their driveways, they needed simply to stick a small red flag in the snow beside their mailboxes, and for a few dollars, the plow would swing in and do a very good job of plowing their driveway. No need for the sorry cobbled together wooden V plows to be dragged behind horses plunging through belly deep snow that had been their "equipment" on the reservation.

Winter sports began to advance to new levels in this new area. Ice skating was very prominent, and weekday-evening social events commonly were skating parties around a tire burning on the ice. Sunday afternoons were often used for ice hockey games which were mostly played by the guys with the girls observing and cheering.

Michael was starting to notice the girls, and they were noticing him as well. He was still processing the dawning realization that he was a person and that there were other people who actually liked to be around him. He was intelligent enough to know immediately after he would commit one of his social gaffes, and while he always learned from his mistakes, there seemed to be a never-ending supply of new ones to make! He was not articulate enough yet to initiate new friendships, and as he witnessed interpersonal blunders made by several young people even more clueless than himself in some areas, he vowed not to make their mistakes. So rather than pursue new friends, he tended to just pick up on overtures made to him, whether male or female. Fortunately, there were some very good kids from both genders who befriended him.

Randy, meanwhile, had his own personal dynamics. He worked hard in school, and he never had to be reluctant to bring home his report card to his mother who would glow with pride in his achievements. Michael sort of felt like Carl Jr. got left off the glory train. He usually got good grades as well, but somehow there was always more fanfare over Randy's achievements. But he knew Randy deserved the praise, it just seemed like Carl Jr. should get a bit more as well.

For his part, Michael tended to pray for miraculous interventions between the school bus ride home and the fateful presentation of the document to his mother. He didn't really care what the intervention was *(bombardment by the Soviet Union or the end of the world would suffice equally well)*—anything to avoid the cold contempt and rebuke from his parents after comparing his grades to his to those of his older brothers! It was an ordeal to be faced every three months.

He knew his travails were self-inflicted, and they all knew he could do so much better with a bit more effort and concentration. But who wanted to use their time in study hall learning about things like square roots, plant roots, and root canals when the time could be put to so much better use by galloping across the prairies and fighting wild Indians with the heroes in the books he read constantly, or even entertaining his fellow study hall hostages with his amusing capers?

Michael was not really what was known as the class clown, but he had a few pranks and sound effects that his classmates really seemed to enjoy. He had suffered from croup and colds so much as a child that he could do tremendous sound effects involving gurgling, slurping mucous. He could also do a racking cough that sounded like his esophagus would surely rip to shreds.

The prank that he enjoyed the most though was whistling through his nose with his mouth totally closed. He had learned to whistle in his throat and let the sound escape through his nostrils. He never could produce much volume, but he could control it enough to actually whistle recognizable tunes. He had to do it intermittently so the study hall teacher could not home in on his location, but the prank amused his classmates to no end! The sound was quiet enough that some study hall teachers let it pass, but some became increasingly frustrated, trying to track down the source. There was one rather chubby middle-aged male teacher who actually seemed impressed by the whistle and would do his best to isolate the source, creating a bit of cat-and-mouse competition between him and Michael. Michael would pretend to be totally absorbed with his studies exhibiting all the right facial expressions as he "studied" but sneak surreptitious glances at the teacher to see where he was looking before sharing the next snatch of Yankee Doodle. Occasionally, he would look up with a bored expression to match the other more normal students. At times, his appropriately dull gaze would meet that of the teacher and move on past to something more interesting such as a blackboard eraser or dictionary.

Then he would allow extra time to pass before Yankee Doodle would continue his ride to town for another few seconds. The biggest challenge for Michael was to maintain his somewhat glazed, bored-out-of-his-skull look when other students were tittering with mirth, and the frustrated teacher sat helpless to stop what he could not identify.

One day, Michael glanced up midperformance to see the chubby teacher staring at him with a knowing half-smile. The smile clearly conveyed the message to Michael that "I know it is you doing it, and I also know there is nothing I can do about it." That ended the game during his study hall sessions. Michael thought the man had worked so hard to figure it out and then handled it so well that he needed to knock it off to respect him.

The inevitable result of all this school time spent reading and entertaining classmates always showed up in the report cards. Carl and Charlotte were not really education enthusiasts, but it irritated them that Michael just wouldn't seriously apply himself like his brothers did. He was always careful, however, to keep his scores high enough to pass to the next grade. To his way of thinking, anything above a passing grade was just "gravy"!

# SMITHVILLE HIGH AND DRIVER'S EDUCATION

Rumors were beginning to circulate about a huge construction project to build a new high school on the banks of the Flambeau river just outside of town. It was to be a three-million-dollar project which in the late 1960s was an enormous expenditure.

Planning for the high school building began in 1967, and to get the project going, after a successful bond issue, eighty acres of land were purchased along the river. The new building would contain nine separate buildings connected by hallways. The plans for the new school were designed for an anticipated future enrollment of a thousand students.

In 1969, the school district established a class offering special services for trainable handicapped children.

The course of studies in high school was changed and arranged to fit the needs of the students for a balanced education, with five main priorities:

1. teaching of Latin
2. teaching of auto mechanics
3. biology class
4. limit home economics to three years
5. a reading program for remedial reading

The school was equipped with excellent facilities for the industrial arts classes such as woodworking, welding and machining, and small motor repair. They offered very good agricultural classes, and it was decided to have physical education with one credit per year and have sixteen credits to graduate—typing outside the regular commercial course and three years of a foreign language.

Perhaps the most advanced addition to the school program was the exciting auto simulators for driver education classes. There were two rows of four simulator booths which were replicas of car interiors from the front seat forward. The steering wheels, shift levers, and all controls as well as gauges gave the operator the same feel as sitting in the driver's seat of a car. There was a huge movie screen in front and a bit above the simulators where very realistic traffic flowed, and the students were to blend in with the traffic and go with the flow. They needed to learn to respond quickly to emergency situations such as cars swerving into their lanes or braking hard in front of them. There were also simulated dangers of pets running out in front of them or a child chasing a ball, etc.

There was a separate booth at the rear of the classroom where the instructor monitored the performance of all simulators. One young man named Tim decided to try to beat the system. Since most infractions were from failure to brake in time, he decided to ride his brake pedal during the whole lesson. Unfortunately for him, the control monitor picked up on that, and he flunked the lesson. It was all very exciting for young people training to get their driving licenses.

The new free study was a radical departure from the highly structured and supervised educational system they had always known. Students would begin the day with assembly in their assigned homerooms where preliminaries such as announcements were made, then they were dismissed to their hour-long class periods. It didn't take long for the rowdier students to take advantage of the greatly reduced supervision. Lovemaking trysts soon developed on the riverbanks, barely concealed by the bushes, and it was common to walk into an unused classroom at any time of day and find couples locked in passionate embraces, even rolling around together on the floor. Surprisingly, nothing was done about this, and once Michael even heard a guy in his class proposition a girl known for her loose morals. They made the arrangement aloud in the classroom. When a thirteen-year-old girl became hugely pregnant and ultimately dropped out of school to have the baby, life went on as usual.

School spirit was something the faculty constantly tried to encourage. Smithville High fielded a reasonably good football team, and on game day, the entire school would assemble in the gymnasium to whip up a good hot fighting spirit in their football jocks. They would sing the school fight song, and then each class from youngest to oldest would stand to shout out the school fight chant. "We're from Smithville, couldn't be prouder. If you can't hear us now, we'll yell a little louder!"

For some reason, school spirit did not exist in Michael's age group. The class directly before them would stand and scream out the chant with red faces and full-throated exultation. The class directly behind would also give a thunderously vociferous account of themselves. But when Michael's class stood, it all came out as some sort of muted confession, offered by self-effacing residents of some ancient monastery!

Each time as the chants progressed up the bleachers toward their class, Michael and his classmates would twitch and start turning red and closely examine the toes of their shoes, knowing full well that they were about to make fools of themselves yet again! It was an unexplainable dynamic that followed them every year through high school.

Coaches for extracurricular activities such as sports and cheerleading also had a difficult time getting their class members to sign up for their activities. The football coach all but drafted a couple of the tougher-looking guys for team tryouts.

Then came the day when the teacher tried to entice some of the girls into trying out for cheerleading. Michael thought there were a few who probably had what it took to paint themselves up and cavort around, scantily clad, screaming chants that would have put Hitler's Brown Shirt Youth troops to shame.

But the girls seemed reluctant to commit themselves, so the teacher coaxed them to at least try out and see if they liked it. Finally, a couple of the girls who were considered the class "hotties" volunteered to try out. Then Michael's gaze landed on a plain-looking Polish girl named Lista Mazinski. She was average in many ways and below average in others, and that, coupled with her Polish heritage, made her a definite class underdog.

Michael saw her eyes shining with her inner imaginations of herself in the esteemed cheerleading squad, and his mind silently pleaded, *No! Don't volunteer! They will mock you right out of the tryouts!*

His heart sank as he saw her timidly raise her hand.

The teacher looked a bit surprised and said, "Lista, are you volunteering?"

Lista nodded her head, her face still alight with excitement.

The teacher turned rather slowly to add her name to the others on the blackboard.

Then it began. Snickers from the class turned into cruel remarks then outright mockery. Michael watched the dream die in her eyes, replaced by a look of horror at what she had dared to do! He hurt for her! He had absorbed his share of mockery and humiliating put-downs to where he knew how and when to keep his head down and his mouth shut. He knew that Lista had too, but for a few short minutes, she had dared to see herself as one of the glamor girls, dancing and shaking her pom-poms.

Now she was shaking her head vigorously from side to side. Her right hand came up with the palm extended as if to ward off a physical blow. "Take it off!" she said, her voice husky and ragged. "Take my name off the list!"

The teacher looked relieved and immediately erased the offending name from the list of "qualified kids." When Michael looked at Lista again, he saw that the excited look on her face had been replaced by her usual plodding dullness.

# SUMMER BATHS

Summer vacations were always busy, and action packed. As soon as school was out for the first summer, Randy was offered a job on a Clayton Mennonite farm owned by a gentle mannered preacher named Luke Manning. They got along well, and Randy enjoyed the work which paid almost nothing, but they provided room and board during the week, and he would go home Friday evenings.

Later that summer, Michael was offered a job by another Clayton Mennonite farmer. The farm was owned by a young married couple named Shem and Rose Skinner, who had several cute young children who were still too small to be of much help around the farm. The pay was a princely sum of three dollars a day.

Shem was a hardworking man who was usually considerate and often fun-loving. His wife was also a fun-loving hard worker but came from a family where bluntness was considered a virtue and your shortcomings were brought to your attention bluntly with little regard for your feelings. This tendency could also rub off on Shem at times, and Michael was occasionally hurt by their corrective rebukes.

One of these occurred when Rose told him one evening during his second week with them that he didn't bathe often enough, and she would like him to take a bath every evening while he was living with them. She very likely had good reason to ask that of him because for the first thirteen years of his life on the reservation, they had had no indoor plumbing or bathroom. Baths were a once-a-week ordeal. Carl would fill a large galvanized tub with warm water, and they would take turns bathing in the same water usually beginning with the oldest to the youngest. It didn't occur to any of them that it might have been a good idea to change the water somewhere in the course of the five sequential baths.

When they had moved to civilization, they had a bathtub, but old habits die hard, and the one-bath-a-week rule still seemed sufficient.

Another time they were taking a break during haying when Rose crawled under the wagon to look at something that didn't seem right. Soon Michael thought he heard her call for him to crawl under and look at it too, so he did. He had just slid under the wagon when she turned on him and said, "Get out of here, Michael. I didn't call for you, I said Shem!"

Hurt and humiliated, he crawled back out and slunk away.

Over the next months, he learned to take their comments without offense, since he came to realize that no offense was intended. In their families, they all talked to each other that way.

Michael was well accustomed to being addressed harshly and demeaned at home, but their involvement in the Glendale church created much interaction with other people who spoke kindly and courteously to each other. This pressured Michael's parents to be more civil to their children, at least when they were with other people. Behind closed doors, however, some extremely unbecoming things continued to occur.

# SMITHVILLE SASH
# AND DOOR

Carl had moved on from working for Laverne to take a job at a door-and-window factory in Smithville. The factory was a set of rather drab buildings near the bank of the Flambeau river. Carl didn't mind the work, but he had a tremendously difficult time accepting the fact that his immediate supervisor was a woman. To make matters worse, she was basically a female version of him!

It was a time when very few women were promoted to supervise men, and she seemed to enjoy it very much. The most difficult thing for him to swallow was the way she would grasp her humble subjects by the arm and march them to where she wanted them to perform their next menial task.

Carl had enjoyed a lifetime of being the unchallenged alpha male and jerking others around. It took all the self-control he could muster to work in that environment, but good jobs were scarce, and the regular paycheck made him hang in there. At times, Michael would be with his mother when she would pick him up after work. They would sit in the gravel parking lot and wait for the howling wail of the day's end whistle, then the doors would open, and a long line of men would come streaming out. Carl was never first in line or last in line but usually could be seen plodding along toward the rear.

While many of the other workers would be laughing and joking around, Carl trudged along in silence with his head bowed, carrying his tin lunch box in his left hand. Much of the freedom he had enjoyed in the past to manage his own life was now gone, and it was hard for him to accept. But his sense of responsibility was strong, and he would have done whatever was required to provide for the physical needs of his family. That was a good characteristic, all his sons would inherit from him.

Carl worked with some very ungodly men, and with his weak character, he was soon dragging home some of their bad attributes and bad language.

One afternoon, he and Charlotte were sitting in the living room enjoying and after work cup of coffee when Eli and Michael got into a spat. Eli was fast becoming the stereotypical spoiled youngest child, and some of his antics and deliberate irritations got to his older brothers.

Suddenly, Carl shouted with a nasty snarl for the boys to come into the living room. Then in front of the family, he ordered Michael and Eli to strip naked except for their T-shirts. Michael was fifteen years of age, and his humiliation was nearly unbearable as he stripped in front of his mother and some of his brothers. Then his father commanded him and Eli to bend over and kiss each other's bare butts. Charlotte gave a nearly inaudible gasp when he issued the order but made no objection. Michael was totally shocked and bewildered that a Christian-professing man could even think of such a filthy punishment, much less carry through with it! Many years later, he would come to the conclusion that his father had probably picked up the idea up at work. Although he would hear that act as a nasty expression all his life, this would be the only time he would ever be forced to actually do it.

Meanwhile, Carl Jr. got a summer job working for Uncle Laverne. The pay was poor, and he got all the unpleasant jobs, but he was earning money, so he hung in there. He was often the recipient of Uncle Lavern's unpleasant and unkind rebukes which he found hard to swallow, but since his father had to live with some of the same treatment, he bit his tongue and soldiered on.

Many of Carl's evenings were spent working on the new addition to the house. It was beginning to take shape, with two stories over a new basement. While Carl's workmanship left much to be desired, he could always figure out how to get the job done. What he lacked in finesse, he made up for in creativity. The boys helped on the project as they could, but chores and schoolwork during that season kept them fairly busy. Michael was very interested in the project. He had never seen a construction project close up, and it was fascinating to see how builders could take a bunch of flat materials and turn it into a building.

# THE GREAT TRACTOR RACE

For the most part, Michael enjoyed working for Shem. Some of the work was rather physically demanding such as dumping one-hundred-pound sacks of cow feed into a wheelbarrow to feed the cows in their tie stalls. He solved that problem by tipping the wheelbarrow up to the feed bag and tying the end of the bag to the handles. When he would pry the handles back down, the sack of feed would follow it and plop nicely into the wheelbarrow bed. He was always on the lookout for other labor-saving ideas. He tied hitch pins to the tractor seats with a length of baler twine string so when it was time to unhook a wagon or implement, it was not necessary to climb down from the tractor seat to pull the pin, but he needed only to give the string a tug and the pin would disconnect.

Shem had two main tractors the first year Michael worked for him. One was a two-cylinder John Deere with a narrow front end, and the other was an Oliver Row Crop model with a narrow front end. Michael was partial to the Oliver since they had had two-cylinder John Deeres all his life, and the Oliver was something different. When he and Shem would pull wagonloads of baled hay home from other farms, they would often race on the road. Michael usually won because his tractor was a tiny bit faster, but occasionally Shem would win with superior driving skills.

One sunny afternoon, they were headed back to the main farm with loads of hay, and Michael was in the lead with the trusty Oliver. He was startled by the roar of the John Deere coming around the passing lane. He made sure the Oliver was wide open, but the John Deere passed him like he was coasting! Michael saw a grinning Shem leaning forward reaching for something as he sailed past, and he was totally confused!

When they arrived back at the barn to unload the hay, Shem refused to give away his secret, and Michael was determined to find it out. In the following days, Shem pulled the same caper on him several more times, and always he would be leaning forward reaching for something.

Finally, one day Michael was working in a field with the John Deere, and he discovered linkage to the tractor's speed governor. When he reached down and pulled it, the engine would speed up uninhibited by the controlling governor. He wondered if the Oliver had a similar setup.

As soon as he found time, he checked the Oliver engine over carefully until he found the speed governor. It was located at the front of the engine, and there would be no way for him to reach it from the seat, so he tied a length of twine string to it and strung it back to where he could reach it from the seat. He kept it out of sight so Shem would not notice it until an opportunity presented itself.

The day finally arrived when he was following Shem and the John Deere back to the barn with loads of hay. He found a long straight stretch of road and moved into the passing lane. He saw Shem watching him out of the corner of his eye as the slightly faster Oliver slowly overtook the John Deere. The length of twine string was hidden in Michael's hand as he awaited the right time. Suddenly he saw Shem reach down for the governor linkage, and he pulled the string to the governor all the way back!

Shem felt the John Deere leap forward, but to his shock, the Oliver was leaping forward as well. They shot down the gravel road neck and neck until Shem finally released the governor and Michael went on around. Michael was proud of himself for his innovation, but Shem said they had better quit overriding the engine governors before they damaged the tractors.

Randy, meanwhile, had damaged a tractor on the Manning farm. He was driving the tractor, which had a front-end loader mounted on it in a muddy area when it began to get stuck. In an attempt to shift the weight to the rear drive tires, he raised the loader to its full height, and when he let it down, it lowered too fast and bent the mount. Instead of the screaming tirade accompanied by a few blows he would have endured had it happened to his father's tractor, Pastor Luke handled it by calmly assuring him it could easily have happened to anyone, and he should not feel bad about it. The older Raptor boys were amazed when Randy shared the story with them.

Michael, however, was experiencing some of the same treatment. While Shem was younger than Pastor Luke and wired with a higher voltage, he was a God-honoring man who did his best to live his faith and raise a godly family. When things went wrong on the farm, he tried to work through it patiently, although his wife found it a bit more difficult.

Michael was fascinated by the modern farm equipment it seemed the farmers all had. The hydraulic loader on the front of the tractor especially captivated him. It was amazing that by simply pumping oil into cylinders, it was possible to generate enough power to lift hundreds or even thousands of pounds! He didn't have occasion to use the loader himself, but whenever he would drive the loader tractor, he would work the boom up and down.

One day, Shem planned to bale hay on a rented field on a neighbor's farm. He sent Michael ahead with two wagons hooked end to end, pulled by the loader tractor. When he got to the field, there were several other pieces of haymaking machinery there already. Since Shem was not there yet, Michael took the opportunity to try out the loader. He carefully placed the bucket under the corner of a hay wagon, and wonder of wonders, it raised effortlessly, taking the wagon gear up with it. He moved on to lift several of the other pieces of equipment, keeping a sharp eye on the road for the cloud of dust that would tell him Shem was arriving.

He felt pretty good that he had stopped playing around before Shem showed up with the tractor and baler. In his mind, the incident was closed. He never noticed Shem's brother-in-law mowing hay the next field over.

Several weeks later, Shem's family attended a family cookout, and that same brother-in-law was there. Michael was roasting a hot dog on a stick with some of the men when the brother-in-law turned to him with a speculative, slightly amused look. "You know," he said, "I had the hardest time trying to figure out what you were doing with that loader the other day, and finally I decided you must just be playing around!"

Michael knew he was busted, and with some amusement, the brother-in-law gave Shem the blow-by-blow account of his loader antics. Shem never rebuked him for his folly, but Michael had a strong sense that he enjoyed his embarrassment!

One summer, Shem bought several new pieces of equipment. First, he bought a new Leyland diesel tractor, and later a new John Deere baler with a bale thrower. Bale throwers were becoming popular because they eliminated the need for farmers to ride the wagons around the field behind the hay balers and stack the hay on the wagons as it came out the back of the baler.

The new bale throwers would eject the bales in a high arc, and they would land in the following wagon. This process required a different type of wagon, however. Standard hay wagons were approximately eight feet wide by sixteen feet long and flat with a backstop frame at the rear. Bale thrower wagons needed tall sides all the way around to contain the unstacked hay bales.

The new bale thrower arrived at the Skinner farm amid much anticipation. They took it out to the hayfield and began to bale hay. It soon became obvious, though, that something was wrong with the bale thrower. The "kicking" mechanism would throw the bale then slam back into position. Shem fiddled with it a bit then called the dealer who sent out a serviceman. The serviceman adjusted everything he could think of but to no avail. He finally offered to take it back into the shop for repairs and furnish an identical "loaner" machine.

The loaner machine worked fine, and in a few days, the new baler was returned, and the loaner taken back to the dealership. The problem, however, had not been fixed. The kicker still slammed back into position. So the dealer was called again, and again he sent out the serviceman to find the problem and fix it. He and Shem spent hours combing over the unit with a fine-toothed comb but could not find a problem.

Michael, however, had noticed one difference between the loaner machine and the new baler. There was a tube-shaped cylinder on each side of the kicker with chrome rods protruding from the ends which went in and out with each bale throw. On the loaner machine, they had been mounted with the wide end down, but on the new one, the wide part was up and the rods down. He doubted that something so simple and so obvious had anything to do with the problem, but hours later, when the frustrated farmer and dealer took a drink break, he finally pointed out the difference to Shem who stared at it for a few seconds in amazement. "Hey!'" he nearly shouted. "I think this little guy has just found the problem!"

Shem pointed the tubes out to the dealer who just shook his head and said, "I can't believe it. Here it was right under our noses, and we couldn't see it!" Shem explained to Michael that the tubes were shock absorbers which were mounted upside down on the new machine so they couldn't work at all. The mechanic turned them around properly, and the machine worked fine.

Michael felt like a hero, especially when he heard Shem tell the story to other farming friends. *Old Albert Einstein had nothing over on him. After all, who really cared whether E=MC squared or not? Understanding how modern farm equipment worked—now that was the thing!*

# COUSIN ELLIE MAE

Michael was riding on the fender of a tractor driven by Shem one day when he poked him and said, "Look what those kids are doing!" They were making their way up a long, winding gravel driveway to a field Shem was renting and were passing the old farmhouse. There were several kids attacking what was intended to be a garden, but the weeds had long since taken dominance over the veggies. The eldest daughter was pushing a lawn mower between the rows to give them access to work on the weeds. She was a tall, willowy girl of about thirteen, and her long hair was braided into two braids which hung down her back.

Michael, who had spent countless hours with his brothers in garden maintenance, had never heard of using a lawn mower as a gardening tool. "That garden is past help," he commented. "Why don't they just let it go?"

"I'm guessing Jake is coming home for a visit," Shem replied, "and if she doesn't have everything up to snuff, he will smack her around!"

Michael stared at Shem, wondering if he was putting him on again. "What are you saying?" he asked, totally confused. "Who are those people? They look like your church people!"

"You ought to know," Shem replied sardonically, "that lady in there is your first cousin! And that's all I'm gonna say about the situation."

Michael's curiosity was piqued, and in the coming weeks, he began to ask about the Ellie Mae Rink family. He didn't go past their house often, but he had never seen a man around the place. That was odd because Mennonite men tended to be very diligent about staying home and providing for their families. There were a few widows with children, but many of them got remarried, so households without men were few and far between.

When Michael asked his mother, she explained how Ellie Mae was his cousin, but she would explain nothing about the lack of a husband and father. Like so many Mennonite secrets that they tried to cover up, the answers came a little at a time. Bits of information trickled in like pieces to a puzzle.

Ellie Mae was a fairly attractive Mennonite girl who had fallen for a man named Jake from outside their circles. He had hung around their church enough to make folks believe he was sincere, then after a few years of marriage, and several kids, he left her and went to live with his new love in the big city. Occasionally, he would find his way back for a short time, and when he came, he would make a big deal out of inspecting her house and grounds-keeping, and if it was not up to his specifications, he would become physically abusive with her. Michael heard stories of how sometimes after Jake had been around, someone from the church would knock on her door, and she would answer it with big bruises on her face.

Over the next few years, Michael would get to know Ellie Mae and her family, and he found them very likeable. They had one young son named Joe who was a lively and fun-loving young boy. One day, the extended Reynolds family was invited to a picnic and ball game at Uncle Laverne's. He had a well-set-up softball diamond, and after dinner, two of the older cousins chose up sides to play ball. During the game, little Joe ran into a swinging bat and was knocked unconscious. He had taken the blow full force to his head, and for a time, they feared for his life. Jake, who was rarely around, was informed of the accident, and he came to see his son in the hospital. He then began making threats to file a lawsuit, but eventually that talk fizzled out. There was simply no one involved who had enough money to be worth the cost of a lawsuit, which tends to be a real downer for litigation!

A few years later, tragedy again struck Ellie Mae's family. Little Joe was out on the gravel road in front of her sister's house when one of the ladies from their church topped the hill in their big family car.

She was unable to stop or avoid him, and once again he was transported to the hospital. But this time, he did not make it out alive.

His death sent huge shock waves through the Mennonite communities in the area. The lady who hit him felt completely awful, but what had happened had happened, and it could not be undone!

# ON THIN ICE

When school began that year, Michael noticed a new kid about his age named Mark. He was kind of cool with a strong build and decent looks. Socially, however, he was a bit backward, and in time he began to interact with Michael until they became fast friends. Michael had never had a best buddy in school before, and he rather liked it. Anyone who hassled one of them had to answer to both of them, and Mark was tough enough that other guys their age didn't really want to test him.

The older, rowdier boys had started getting their kicks by hanging smaller kids on the flagpole hook where the rope was wrapped. It was about four feet off the ground, and they would hang their victims by the back of their belts, leaving them kicking and twisting helplessly in midair. The pranksters found this extremely amusing, and Michael might well have been a candidate for this treatment had he not been buddies with Mark, who people didn't want to mess with.

There were dark rumors about Mark's background which further discouraged older kids from harassing him. For his part, Mark seemed to enjoy Michael's way with words and storytelling abilities. They were inseparable for most of the school year. Then toward the end of the year, Mark met him on the playground one day and said, "Well, I guess we are done being friends now."

Michael stared at him in bewilderment. "What are you talking about?" he asked, confused and hurt.

"I'm talking about us," Mark replied. "No one can be friends forever."

"Are you upset at something I said or did?" Michael asked, trying to make sense of it all.

"No," Mark responded, "you didn't say or do anything, we are just done being friends! Friendships can't last forever." With that, he turned and walked out of Michael's life.

Michael was deeply hurt by that rejection, and in the weeks to come as he became better friends with some of the other guys, he noticed Mark hanging around the school and playground by himself. When he got past the hurt and rejection, he began to feel kind of sorry for Mark.

Then one day, many weeks later, Mark walked up to Michael and suggested that they be friends again. "No," Michael responded, "we tried that once, and it did not end well." There was a big part of him, however, that very much wanted to be best friends with Mark again. But he knew it would only invite future heartache.

Besides that, Michael was starting to be included in a group of about a half dozen boys who had their own thing going. It was the closest thing to a gang Smithville had at the time, although no one was aware of that. They dreamed up their own brand of fun and excitement—some of it illegal, and all of it unacceptable.

But Michael felt an empowerment when he hung around with them even though he knew he was skating on very thin ice!

One day, he found several of the guys huddled in the coat room comparing something. When he asked them what they were doing, they showed him some merchandise they had shoplifted during lunch hour.

Students were allowed to walk up town with permission during noon lunch hour. These boys had made a game of seeing who could steal the most value in merchandise over the lunch hour. They had gotten their mothers to sew pockets inside their jackets toward the bottom where they would smuggle the stolen property out of the store.

Michael struggled with this for a while but noticed the guys were a bit cooler toward him the longer he refused to participate. Finally, he asked his mother to sew him a special pocket inside his jacket and actually sold her on the idea to where she complied. The next day, he proudly showed the new pocket to his friends, and he was in the shoplifting business.

The game they played terrified him! But it also gave him certain thrills that he had never experienced. The stakes were so high that the consequences of getting caught were unimaginable! Many of the things they stole were of no use to them. The game was about combined dollar value. The largest thing Michael stole was a box of automotive spark plugs from a hardware store. He never won the contest for highest dollar value, but he came close that day. No one had any use for the spark plugs, so he threw them in the trash at school.

It wasn't long until Michael's conscience began to bother him with increasing intensity. He knew stealing was wrong, and doing it as a gang did not make it any more acceptable.

He was riding with Grandpa Raptor around town one day to do some errands when his grandfather told him to stay in the car a few minutes while he ran into the hardware store. He was carrying a staple gun in his hand. When he climbed back into the car, he held up the staple gun with a slight smile and said, "Now this is mine! I could have had it for free because the other day I accidentally carried it out of the store and forgot to pay for it, and nobody noticed!"

As he reached for the ignition key, he looked across at a rather confused Michael and said, "But I ain't selling my soul to the Devil for eleven bucks!"

One evening after school, Michael confessed it all to his horrified mother. The next day at noon, she met him at the school and she went with him to every store where he had shoplifted and he confessed to each store manager and paid for the stolen items with a sincere apology. One of the managers told him to be sure to include the sales tax, which he thought was kinda weird. How do you account for sales tax on stolen merchandise?

When everything he could remember had been made right, Michael felt a huge sense of relief and freedom. Although his parents were not the kind who would pray with him to make sure things were right with God, Michael sought God's forgiveness and believed he was made free from the ugliness of what he had done. He was never again tempted to steal for any reason. Years later as a businessman, his suppliers would make thousands of dollars' worth of errors in his favor, but he always corrected the mistakes for them and paid the difference.

His mother, however, never forgot what he had done and occasionally brought it up to him for the rest of her life. When he was hurt or offended by her refusal to lay it down, he would remind himself that it was after all reaping for the seeds that he had sown. His relationship with his mother had never been anywhere near close and continued to deteriorate as time went on.

Michael was fighting fierce inner battles from the old life on the reservation, and the few times he had tried to open up to her about his demons from the past, she had belittled and criticized him until he had finally learned to keep his problems to himself. He was also often hurt and humiliated when his parents made jokes about him being the family "fat boy" and how he was so naughty that all his life he had needed at least one "spanking" each day!

He also struggled with a deep-seated anger over how his mother would tell people that he didn't know how to run. She had extrapolated that theory from the time she had looked out the window and seen the boys running and playing while Michael had been hopping sideways clacking his shoes together. From inside the house where she had been watching, she was not able to hear the clopping sound of his shoes smacking together. which sounded like a horse galloping. He hadn't been trying to run, he was making horse sounds. But in spite of seeing him run hundreds of times after that, she told people for the rest of her life that he had never known how to run.

# "Bend Your Back!"

As school and church life led to more and more social opportunities for the boys, Carl and Charlotte found it increasingly difficult to maintain their iron control over every aspect of their lives. Carl Jr. was fast becoming a young man, and he chafed under his parents' micromanagement. Randy had a more pliable nature and his mother's favor, which made him a less confrontational child, but Michael was just an ongoing "problem child." He had a quick wit and tended verbalize his thoughts before his mind could even begin to engage a filter. His thoughts were often not what his parents wanted to hear, costing him many blows to the face and mouth. With Carl away working days, it fell mostly to Charlotte to beat him into submission. There was absolutely no sense of humor allowed and zero tolerance for wisecracks. She began to beat his mouth with a rubber spatula. She continued doing this for months, creating a lifelong phobia in him about getting hit in the face.

Michael hated himself for being so quick to verbalize things that were obvious to all but unlawful to mention. There just seemed to be so many opportunities to inject humorous and sometimes sarcastic comments! He always enjoyed sarcastic humor even when it was deployed at his expense.

One evening at supper, Charlotte announced that some of her sisters had invited her to go on a trip with them. The Raptor boys had long been talking among themselves about how much time their mother spent running around with her sisters and slanted sidelong glances at each other at this announcement. Michael had a wisecrack he couldn't resist, despite this being a wisecrack-free zone. "By all means, go," he deadpanned. The words had been still in the air when the back of Carl's hand found his mouth.

Michael had come by his wisecracks honestly. His mother had a quick wit and was constantly saying things that belittled her naughty boys. She would order them to clean the living room, then sit in her armchair, and micromanage their efforts. *"Bend your back!"* she would order them imperiously as they dragged the vacuum across the floor. This would accompany a long list of similar instructions, which would leave the boys fuming with frustration.

These frustrations would be vented when she would be gone, leaving the boys with orders to clean the house before she returned. One boy would be running the vacuum while the others (especially Johnny) would shout, *"Bend your back!"*

Charlotte was sharp enough to catch on when her sons' frustrations reached the red zone. She tried various tactics to ratchet down tension levels—perhaps the least effective of which involved her passive-aggressive tactics. She didn't realize that she was too strong a personality to pull that maneuver off successfully and ended up providing her young charges with even more mimic-worthy material that they would parody for years. Like dissolving into tears with loud boo-hoo-hoos and rushing into her bedroom to kneel by her bed and pray for her errant children. She made sure, of course, to kneel in front of the open door where they could see her and be stricken with guilt.

There was also the (intended) soul-smiting comments, delivered with gut-wrenching pain in her voice and eyes filled with agony. "I do my best to please you boys and all you do is fuss!" Or the somewhat less eloquent "If that's how you want to treat your mother...," which usually trailed off to allow their minds to reach horribly obvious ramifications!

These theatrics were of special interest to young Johnny, who had always been the master irritating sound effects and one-liners. One of his favorites was to stare at one of his brothers who was getting upset and make a sizzling *zzzz* sound. If that failed to contribute to their displeasure, sometimes he would embellish it by licking his finger and holding it close to their necks, as if checking the temperature under their collar. His success rate at helping their temperature rise was near one hundred percent!

He not only was good at coming up with original material, he had a tremendous sense of timing to inject recycled quotations. Many times, when on the receiving end of a verbal beat-down from his older brothers, he would look at them with big sad eyes and say, "I do my best to please you boys, and all you do is fuss!" The humor of this perfectly timed quote would often defuse the gravity of his offense.

# WHEN NATURE CALLS

Charlotte was becoming increasingly frustrated with her middle son for various reasons, and Michael was very aware of it. He wasn't sure why everything he said or did seemed to irritate her so much, often to where she would hit him, but he just assumed there must be something rotten about him.

While she was trying to fix him by kicks to the tailbone and lots of face-slapping, he was starting to seek revenge in small, subtle acts of sabotage.

One day during summer vacation, she left for town and instructed him to iron large stack of clothes before she returned. Since the boys had no sister, they were required to learn to do house chores as well as farming chores.

Struggling with bitterness and frustration, Michael sat and stared at the stack of clothes to be ironed while she was out with her sisters. It was a beautiful afternoon, and he wanted so much to be out riding horseback, but here he sat, looking at his afternoon in the form of a huge stack of clothes to be ironed.

He sat there fuming inside until nature began calling him. Suddenly, an arguably brilliant idea occurred to him. He was supposed to iron the clothes. The iron was a steam iron. Steam irons required water. Mother nature was asking him to discharge some water!

He filled the iron with the yellow water and began to press the clothes. Somehow the odious job was almost fun that day. It didn't occur to him until much later that the whole family had to pay for his payback stunt.

While Michael escaped retribution for this stunt, he was not as fortunate in a related transgression. In the months before the upstairs bathroom was functional, relieving one's bladder required a tedious trip downstairs, where as often as not, the bathroom would be occupied. It was much easier to simply raise the window sash and let gravity take its course.

This policy served him well until the day his mother was looking directly out the living room window when suddenly the object of her attention was blurred by a strange yellow rain! It took her all of a half-second to discern the functional dynamics of the situation and call her son down for a verbal scourging.

Although he was rather embarrassed about it, Michael shared the story with Leighton. To his surprise, Leighton was totally unfazed. "Oh, I've done that for years," he asserted. "I never got caught until the screen started to rust out!"

Another bedroom related incident was centered around the boys" total lack of comprehension of the need for keeping bedrooms clean and tidy. *What was the point of making up a bed when you are just going to crawl back in and mess it up again? And how do clothes lying on the floor become less functional than clothes on hangers? Sure, if the dirt on the floor gets thick enough to show footprints, it would be necessary to sweep said floor, but the fact is that floors are for walking on, not eating off of. It stands to reason that anything you walk on is going to get dirty, so why get all sweat up about a little dust and dirt on the floor?*

That was how Michael reasoned, but his mother's logic took an entirely different path. *Boys have lots of energy, so why not expend a portion of it keeping their room clean?*

Predictably, Carl would weigh in with his overreactive threats and warnings, of which his favorite seemed to be "If you kids don't get that room cleaned up, I'm gonna go up and spread straw on the floor. If you want to live like pigs, I'll bed you down like pigs!"

Michael was convinced that was an empty threat, but sure enough, one evening, the boys entered their bedroom and discovered a small pile of straw in the corner of the room. It was a very small pile, less than two feet in diameter and several inches high. Randy burst out laughing, and Carl Jr. just sort of rolled his eyes heaven-ward without saying much.

Michael thought it was just about as pathetic a stunt as he had seen in a while! If you want to make a point, use a serious demonstra-tion. This was nothing more than a weenie illustration, and he fig-ured it was so their father could go around and tell all his friends and associates about the hilarious lesson he had taught his messy kids. But the story did amuse their friends and relatives, so Michael, who understood the value of a good story or joke, didn't let it irritate him.

# BARGAINING
# WITH JOHNNY

Horseback riding had always been a near daily activity for the older Raptor boys. Johnny, however, was not as into it as the rest of them. He was a capable rider but just not that enthused about riding. Michael often wondered if there was anything on earth that Johnny was enthused about. They had had the same frustration with him about riding bicycle. He had a more low-key personality and was content to just sit around and read books or gaze into space. The older boys had harassed and physically forced him into learning to ride, but even after he learned to ride, it was not on his list of preferred activities.

It was the same with horseback riding. He had learned to ride, but it seemed like an unnecessary expenditure of his limited supply of energy. This was often frustrating to Michael who all but lived on horseback.

Randy had always been his most willing and faithful riding partner, but as he got older and spent more time away from home, Michael had to rely on his unmotivated younger brother to ride with him. He often had to threaten, bargain, and cajole Johnny to accompany him, then when he did go along, he was content to plod along at the speed of the average tortoise.

Michael was all about speed and racing, and he never had to convince his older brothers to compete with him.

Randy's horse Dusty, however, was developing some bad habits. He would at times stubbornly refuse to run at all and just plod along at a walk no matter how his rider would beat him.

His other bad habit was much more dangerous. He would be racing down the gravel road at full speed and veer off ninety degrees into a driveway, sometimes sending his rider flying off his back at a high rate of speed. The older boys had learned to watch for that when they raced him, but Johnny didn't ride him that often.

The older boys had their own saddles, but Johnny did not own one yet and seemed in no hurry to acquire one. Michael owned two saddles—the western style saddle that he used regularly and an odd army surplus saddle from the US Cavalry. He was proud of the cavalry saddle but didn't use it much because it sat different than the western saddles he was used to and felt rather uncomfortable.

One lazy afternoon, Michael decided to go riding. With both his older brothers gone, he began to try to convince Johnny to join him. It took all his powers of persuasion, but he finally convinced him to go along. It irritated Michael that his little brother was such a shrewd bargainer. A capitalist before his time, Johnny nearly always turned a request into a negotiation and usually came out of it with something to enrich his daily existence.

When the negotiations concluded that day, they headed for the barn to saddle their mounts. Johnny chose to ride Dusty and Michael saddled Twinkle for himself.

They walked and jogged the horses several miles to the river and spent some time riding through the graveyard at the river's edge. Michael was a bit bored by the slow pace, so when they turned the horses toward home, he decided to speed things up a bit.

"Hey, Johnny," he proposed, "how about a race to the woods?"

"Naw," Johnny replied without enthusiasm. "What would be the point? We all know that Dusty is the fastest horse on the farm."

"Well, let's just race for fun," Michael responded. "Come on, don't be a stick in the mud!" He was disgusted by his brother's lack of enthusiasm for anything that required the expenditure of physical effort.

"Johnny," he barked, "you are gonna hafta toughen up and learn to apply yourself or you will end up a soft little pansy with an office job some day!"

Without warning, Johnny dug his heels into the buckskin's ribs, and he leaped down the road with Michael and the black mare in hot pursuit. Michael bent low over the mare's mane as the stones and gravel flew from the horses' pounding hooves and the wind whipped through their manes. The euphoria of the race had his senses singing until an awful thought hit him. They were approaching a neighbor's driveway where Dusty had several times swerved in at full speed and unloaded his rider. The older boys had learned to put the other horse on that side of the road when they raced to keep him going straight. But they had not lined up for the race, and the buckskin was on the wrong side! Twinkle was not fast enough to come around behind and come back up alongside him before they got to the driveway.

A horrified Michael knew exactly what was coming and was powerless to stop it! The dynamics of the coming calamity were even worse than he realized. The neighbors' driveway was shaded by huge pine trees and the winter's thick layer of ice on it could take weeks or even months to completely melt away. There was still a layer of ice there when the buckskin thundered into his ninety degree turn at full speed. His unshod hooves hit the ice, and he immediately went down hard on his side, pinning Johnny's leg and foot under him as he slid on his side toward the bushes. When his rocketing slide was finally stopped by the trees and bushes, the horse scrambled to his feet again, but his rider lay pale and motionless in the bushes.

Sick with an icy fear, Michael dragged his horse to a sliding stop and was off and running toward his brother before she came to a full stop! Michael knelt beside him not even sure if he was alive or dead! "Johnny," he said, shaking him gently, "are you okay?"

Johnny seemed to come back to full consciousness, and there was a terrible pain in his foot! "My foot!" he groaned. "I think it's broken!"

Michael, relieved that he was alive, ran to the neighbor's house to call his mother. He then returned to Johnny's side to wait for her to come with the car. As he thought it all over, he knew that he was responsible for goading Johnny into a race that he hadn't wanted. Michael also knew that when Johnny related the story to their parents, Carl would fly into a rage and beat him savagely!

"Johnny," he said, "I'm sorry! You can't tell Mom and Dad that I made you race. They won't be mad if it's just a riding accident!"

His little brother just looked up at him, the pain showing in his eyes, and said nothing.

"Johnny!" Michael pleaded. "Promise me you won't tell them!"

Michael never knew if his brother's mind was hazy or if he was just being a little crippled capitalist. "I'll give you my cavalry saddle if you don't tell them," he pleaded.

"Okay," Johnny croaked, and the deal was done.

Johnny was true to his word, and the official story of what had happened never included the incriminating details. When Johnny returned from the hospital, hopping on crutches, he was the proud owner of a cavalry saddle in real decent condition. Many years later when they were both grown men, he told Michael, "By the way, there was no way I would have ever told the folks what happened out there. You could have kept your saddle and been completely safe! But since you offered..."

# A Kick to the Rear and Spotlight Sports

One day, Michael spent a bit too much time in the bathroom. There was always reading material strategically placed within reach of the commode, and all of them liked to read while they roosted. Randy claimed it was the most comfortable chair in the house, although there was some debate on that declaration.

That day, Charlotte warned Michael to get out so others could use it, but he was in the middle of a good article and wanted to finish it. Charlotte never allowed any of them to lock the bathroom door for any reason, whether they were using the toilet or bathing. She also never allowed shower curtains, and when they moved into a house that already had them, she immediately took them down. It bugged the boys how she would pop in any time she felt so inclined.

After the second warning, Michael heard the thumping of her slippered feet marching toward the bathroom, so he hurriedly jerked up his trousers and scurried out the door. As he scampered through the door, his mother was waiting around the corner to "love on him" with her foot. In her anger, she wound up and delivered a mighty kick to his behind. But she hadn't taken into account that she was wearing her soft bedroom slippers instead of her hard shoes. Her son felt very little impact, but Charlotte's big toe broke on impact, and she let out a howl of pain.

In the following days, it turned purple and green and swelled to half again its normal size. Although they couldn't show the slightest hint of the glee, they freely expressed to each other in private, she seemed to catch on to her sons' enjoyment of her misfortune and decided to try to milk the situation on the premise that mothering them was so hard. She would display the traumatized digit when most of the family was together and say things like "If I as your mother need to suffer some pain to help you boys learn, I am willing to do that for you!" Mahatma Ghandi would have been so proud of her! To be willing to suffer so much pain for a poorly executed kick to her son's rear was indeed remarkable, the boys agreed in private then hooted with laughter!

The high points of the boys' existence were mostly centered around their social lives. In the years before Carl Jr. acquired his own wheels, Cousin Henry would faithfully pick them up in whatever death trap on wheels he happened to be driving at the time and haul them off to the appointed social event. He usually made the drive interesting as well with his humorous stories or wild rides on ice covered roads. Often at night, the handheld spotlight would come out, and they would scan the roadside ditches and fields for deer and other wildlife. Deer were plentiful, and they would light up whole herds grazing in hay fields. The deer would stand mesmerized by the bright light until they passed.

One night, when they were all packed in Henry's car headed back from a youth social event, someone dug out the high-powered spotlight and began shining for deer.

The social event had been held in one of the homes way back in the sticks, and the light was soon revealing abundance of wild game, especially deer. They could not have known that some unfortunate young man had been hiking along that same gravel road when mother nature began making the kind of demands on him that required him to climb part way up the hill beyond the ditch and drop his drawers to take care of business. As Henry's car rounded the bend, the blazing spotlight scored a direct hit on his pale behind. The poor fellow scrambled around for a bit, not sure what his best option was. All his instincts told him to cover his behind, but to do so, he would need to stand and pull up his pants, thus providing even more of a show.

He finally tried to lean forward in somewhat of a standing crouch to pull them up his pants and managed to provide even more subject matter to the uncompromising glare of the spotlight.

The young fellow obviously hoped they would pass quickly, but that was not to be! Henry coasted the car to a near stop, rolled down his window, and shouted, "*I spy!*" then roared away in a shower of gravel. His ridiculous response to the plight of the unfortunate young victim had them laughing the rest of the way home.

# THE HOCKEY RINK

Ice hockey was a very big deal to their youth group. They played on ponds, rivers, and wherever they could find smooth enough ice. Their goal posts eventually evolved from a stick laid flat on the ice, to burlap covered frames, compliments of Cousin Henry and his brothers-in-law. Henry had married into somewhat of a maverick Mennonite family who didn't really care for the long lists of rules governing most Mennonite churches. His father-in-law, Larry Bannon, was a God-fearing, church-going man, but he governed his family with a heavy hand where respect and obedience were concerned but a rather light touch regarding social mores and church rules. His wife Katlin had a more gentle and compassionate nature.

They were a good-looking and very athletic family and skilled in hunting and fishing as well as nearly every sport that interested them.

Henry had his hands full competing against his older brothers-in-law, Ralph, the oldest of the boys, and his younger brother Brian.

One cold winter Saturday morning when Carl was gone, Cousin Henry showed up at the Raptor house in his clunky old pickup truck. I need the boys to help me on a project he announced to Charlotte. Somehow, he had a way of making her cooperative where the boys were concerned. It might have been his high-powered personality or his fun-loving bonhomie, but she usually let the boys go with him. Once, when they were explaining to him how she liked to use social functions to control them, he exclaimed, "Well, what for an old battle axe, is she?" It was typical Henry-speak, and as usual, it cracked the boys up with laughter.

They all piled into his truck, and they roared away over the snow packed roads. "We are gonna go pick up a load of sawmill slabs and make a hockey rink," he announced. The Raptor boys had never heard of an ice-skating rink and had absolutely no idea what he had in mind. But they knew that whatever happened, with Cousin Henry, it would be an adventure.

An hour and a half later, they met Ralph and Brian at the intended location of the new ice rink. Henry began issuing instructions, and they spread the wood slabs around in a large circle. The slabs were approximately ten feet long and were flat on one side but curved on the other. They were the piece that remained after the sawmill had sawed round logs into flat boards.

When the slabs were all spread around, Henry and the Bannon boys began nailing them together to create a short wall approximately eight inches high. Carl Jr. had enough construction experience that he was able to understand their plan. Randy was slowly catching on too, but Michael was totally at a loss and trying to gain some understanding with a barrage of questions.

"How do you expect those crooked boards to hold the water in?" he asked.

"They don't hold the water in," Henry retorted. "The water freezes."

"Well, how are you going to get water in it when there is no pond or creek?" he wondered.

"We're gonna pump it in with a hose" was the response.

"How are you going to keep the water from freezing in the hose?" was the next question.

"Running water doesn't freeze" was the exasperated reply.

"Well, how are you gonna get it deep enough to skate on it without it running through the cracks in the boards?" Michael asked, still not comprehending the master plan.

By now, Ralph had had enough of this ignorant kid. "We are gonna skate on it!" he said. "It doesn't have to be deep enough to fall in!" Everyone except Michael thought that was very funny.

He finally figured out that the slab boards were for keeping the hockey puck on the ice, not for holding water in. It seemed to him that that could have been explained right away and saved all the incomprehension! But if it gave them all a good laugh, it was okay.

It was all moot anyway because the rink never saw a drop of water, frozen or otherwise.

Michael was always glad when the Bannon kids came to youth activities for several reasons. One reason was that they were a lot of fun and always helped keep things lively. Another was that he loved to watch their athletic skills in play.

Another rather significant reason he liked it when they came was that they had a rather attractive girl about his age who seemed to return his personal interest. Michael was beginning to get quite interested in girls, and for reasons he never really understood, they returned his interest. In time, this would play a huge and defining role in his life, but for now the Raptor rule seemed to be not only no dating before eighteen years of age but no interest either. His parents could dictate and regulate his actions, but there was no way they could dictate his interests. And like several of his brothers, Michael had learned to share absolutely nothing of consequence with his parents, in spite of Charlotte's many efforts to trick information out of them.

Somehow this rule didn't really apply to Randy though. He had taken quite an interest in the pastor's younger daughter, Rene, who was actually closer to Michael's age. She was an energetic, vivacious blonde who gave a good account of herself in contact sports in spite of competing against mostly guys.

Given their mediocre-at-best athletic abilities, the Raptor boys were quick to appreciate it in others. This was one of the things that attracted Randy to her. Once, in a school assignment, his class was to list the characteristics that attracted them to the opposite sex. He listed athletic ability very high which earned him some ribbing from his classmates. One guy asked him loud enough for the whole class to hear whether he was looking for a girlfriend or a quarterback!

Both of the Miller girls had a great relationship with their parents and called their dad papa. Unfortunately for Randy, Rene had a very high-pitched voice which could get squeaky when she was animated. Michael and Johnny had great fun embarrassing Randy by mimicking her voice. It was usually done in fun, but not always.

The Raptor brothers had their share of fights among themselves, especially Randy and Michael. Ironically, Randy and Michael were the closest to each other in age and interaction, but it seemed they also had the most conflict. Michael struggled with anger and bitterness from their past life and would give vent to his anger when goaded or mocked by his brothers.

Once, however, he discovered a different way to hand it back to big brother who was by now an official item with Rene. Randy was mocking him about the tired old fat line and Michael was heating up fast.

Suddenly in front of his other brothers, Michael turned real calm and serious and stared at Randy for a long minute. "Randy," he squealed in a perfect imitation of Rene's squeaky voice, "Papa says it's not nice to make fun of other people!" He was rewarded to see his brother actually turn a bit red as he walked away.

Sometime later when Randy was working with Cousin Paul, he told him that Rene had been voted in for song leader at the Glendale church. "Oh boy!" Paul said laughing. "That will have the old men clearing their throats!"

# YOUTH RALLY

One of the great highlights of their social existence was travelling to Minnesota for the annual winter youth rallies. A small Mennonite mission church there sponsored Bible-based social programs to which their youth group was invited. The sponsoring pastor and his family were longtime fast friends with the Raptors because his wife had been a close friend of Charlotte in their youth, and they had maintained contact over the years. Carl Jr. found it especially interesting because it was their daughter who was his current romantic interest. Ironically, this was also the place where the incredible spiritual revival events had begun which had culminated in the South Dakota reservation chapel where the Raptor boys were born and spent their early years.

Michael especially enjoyed it because it was an opportunity to get away from his parents hyper-control. The facility was rustic to the point of crude. In the early years, the pastor and his wife hosted the girls in their large house while the boys were housed in the nearby garage where rough bunks had been made for them to sleep. The rustic accommodations blended in nicely with the wild beauty of the northern woodlands. The Bible lessons and social events occurred at the nearby church which had a large basement with kitchen facilities. The organizers of these events did a fine job of putting together interesting Bible study topics and an even better job of selecting interesting pastors and teachers to address them. It was one of the local pastors named Lee who elicited high praise from Randy.

Randy always claimed that when he heard this pastor preach, the realization hit him for the first time that there is no standard requirement for sermons to be long, dry, and boring, and that there were some (although few it seemed) pastors who actually had something useful to share and had the ability to make it interesting! Pastor Lee never rose to any lofty positions of acclaim, but he served a long and very useful life as a minister worth listening to.

Music was always a big part of the youth rallies, and the Glendale youth fit right in with all their gifted singers and musicians. As they would sit around a crackling campfire singing to the guitars and other instruments, Michael wanted to be able to play guitar more than anything else in the world. He sat spellbound as the accomplished guitar pickers like Leon brought their guitars to life and the music flowed. Yet, in spite of countless hours poring over the various books and trying to coax music out of his guitar, he made no progress.

Recorders and microphones were becoming more popular, and at one rally, the program included grouping all the kids by age and having each age group come to the front of the chapel to sing a special song for the rest of the group. This was no sweat for Michael because his age group was fairly well represented and included several of the talented Kurtz kids. When they were called to the front to do their song, Michael noticed that there were several cords strung from the back of the chapel to the front to power the equipment being used for this very special occasion. They sang their song and returned to their seats, and Michael thought they had given a pretty good account of their age group.

The next age group called up included Randy and Leighton Stevens who were sitting together on the bench behind Michael and Donnie. When their group was summoned, Randy and Leighton stood rather reluctantly and looked around to see who would be joining them. Nobody else stood. They turned a nice shade of pink and began a slow sinking motion back to their bench, but the event leader called out, encouraging them to come forward and sing a duet.

The outgoing Leighton was less intimidated than his buddy Randy, so he stood back up and headed for the front of the church, followed by the hapless Randy whose pink complexion was darkening to a nice shade of red. Unfortunately, he was too nervous and embarrassed by the situation to notice the cords underfoot, and his toe went under them and nearly sent him sprawling. He clutched at the end of a chapel pew to keep from falling, and after a bit of a recovery dance not unlike a chicken on crack, he resumed full vertical posture and emitted a loud and very high-pitched, girlie giggle.

In years to come, Michael would not be able to remember what song they sang. He would not remember who all was and wasn't at that youth rally or who spoke on what subject. He would not remember what activities they had enjoyed. But the sound of that ludicrous girlie giggle in that quiet chapel would stay with him forever! And every time he thought about it, he would laugh out loud!

# MILKING COWS AND BUYING HAMBURGER

Back on the farm, Carl had decided to milk cows again. He and his young servants cleaned out a part of the tumbledown barn, and he bought some cows and milking equipment.

It would be many years before Michael would hear the cliché that "the definition of insanity is doing the same thing over and over and expecting a different result," but he had ample opportunities to witness this play out in real life. The cows were a ton of work and aggravation and provided an ounce of income. The barn was drafty, and cows got sick. One of the cows cut her back leg on some of the junk in the barnyard, and it got infected. Carl tried cleaning and disinfecting it, but it would not heal. One night, he decided to try a "natural" poultice he had heard about. He prepared a rag bandage and applied a liberal amount of the poultice to the rag which he then tied around the infected area.

The cow died. Carl was somewhat mystified as to why she died, but Michael was pretty sure it was directly related to the "natural" poultice, which was in fact pure cow manure!

The next summer, Carl decided to tear down his barn and build a new one. They would salvage as many of the boards from the old barn as possible. When they had taken everything useable, a call was made to Brian the excavator, who showed up a few days later with his bulldozer and knocked down the barn hill and buried what was left of the old barn. The boys lamented the passing of the barn hill because when the winter snows were deep, they would hook old car hoods or toboggins behind their horses on long ropes, then gallop the horses around the base of the hill bringing the homemade sled sailing through the air as it crested the hill at a high rate of speed.

Having had horses all their lives, the Raptor boys were always looking for ways to get creative with them as power sources. Flying over the crest of the old barn hill had always been good for a thrill.

The hill was not completely eliminated, but the steep part was graded down to a gradual swell upon, which the new barn would sit.

The new barn resembled a garage more than a barn. It was a simple frame structure with a peak roof and sided with plain plywood. Carl decreed that it would be painted red because barns are red. So he went shopping for paint.

Carl never really explained how he ended up with the ultra-bright shade of red that he purchased, but it almost glowed in the dark. It was a brighter shade of flaming red than the average fire engine and did absolutely nothing to enhance a barn-like image. But it was fairly well constructed, and the unproductive cows did not complain.

It was not long until everyone was sick of the cows. They were all sold off except one, which was kept for milk.

While there may be a certain nostalgic appeal to having a milk cow around for the family's daily needs, she proved to be a very large thorn in their sides. Twice a day, she had to be milked and that by hand. Someone would be appointed to take a stainless-steel bucket and rope out to the pasture and tie old Betsy to whatever was handy and extract her twice daily offering, one squirt at a time. It was a huge inconvenience to save pennies a day on milk, and finally Carl wised up and turned her into steaks and hamburger.

One day, after the last bite of old Betsy had been digested, Michael was accompanying his mother on some errands around town which included grocery shopping. Michael was not much of a shopper, but it was handy for Charlotte to have her own pack mule to haul her purchases to the car. The final stop of the day was at the grocery store, and when the last bulging bags had been stowed in the back seat of the family sedan, Charlotte was putting the key in the ignition when she paused and said, "Oh no, I forgot the hamburger!"

She extracted some money from her purse and shoved it at Michael with instructions to hurry back in and buy some hamburger. Michael had never in his life bought groceries, but *how hard could it be! Go to the meat counter, grab some hamburger, pay for it, and pop back out!*

To his surprise, none of the large selection of meat packages on display was labeled hamburger. He carefully examined all the meats on display, roasts, steaks, sausages, ground beef, and other selections but found no hamburger. When he was convinced that there was no hamburger available, he went back out to the car where his frustrated mother was wondering what had been taking him so long.

"They don't have any hamburger" he reported confidently as he returned her money. He was secure in the knowledge that he had done his "due diligence."

Charlotte looked hat him in disbelief! "No hamburger?" she exclaimed. "They *always* have hamburger!"

"I looked very hard," her son reported, "and there was not one pack of hamburger."

"Did you ask someone from the store?" Charlotte asked, rather peeved at her wasted time.

Michael stared at her with the deer in the headlights look. It had simply not occurred to him that he could just ask for assistance! "No," he mumbled, "I never thought of that."

Charlotte gave her head a slow shake of incredulity at her clueless son, then put the car in gear, and headed for home. Somewhere on the way, a thought hit her, and her gaze snapped from the roadway to her son. "You *do* know that hamburger is called ground beef, don't you?" she asked testily.

"It is?" he responded, surprised. "They had lots of ground beef, I was looking for hamburger like you said!"

# WELDERS, GO-CARTS, AND PUPPY LOVE

Michael was for the most part enjoying working summers for Shem. Shem's wife was from a large family most of whom were married with families living in the same area and doing the same thing—farming. One of her sisters named Annie was married to a Doug Byler, and their family interacted with Shem's family a lot, so Michael got to know them fairly well. Doug had a reputation as a hard-driving, no-nonsense workaholic, and he owned two farms as did several men in their church.

One evening, Shem's family was invited over to Doug's place after chores for a picnic and to spend the evening. Michael was rather confused when during the milking chores, Shem proposed that he act real smart-aleck and sassy to him in front of Doug and his wife that evening. One thing the Raptor boys had had literally hammered into them was never to deliberately disrespect their elders, and he was very hesitant, but Shem strongly urged him to do it to see what Doug and Annie would say afterward. Michael would never understand why Shem would ask that of him unless he wanted people to think that his hired man was a real problem to control.

The fiasco was muted by Shem's inability to stay serious during the exchange, and in the end, it fell flat.

One of their nearest neighbors were the Lars Svenson family who lived about a mile and a half south of them on the gravel road. They were a Swedish family with an only son named Thad who was Michael's age. Thad made more of an effort to be friends with Michael than Michael reciprocated. It wasn't that Michael didn't like Thad, he did. But they did not have a lot in common. His older brothers liked Thad a lot though, due largely to the fact that Thad

had free access to the welder his father kept stored in an old refrigerator by the back-porch door.

In the days before they finally got their own welder, the Raptor boys were on a constant quest to build a real, functional go-cart. Carl Jr. was by now convinced that such an undertaking would not be possible without having access to a welder. Thad was fairly generous in sharing the welder with them as well as scraps of steel from the large pile of scrapped farm equipment by their garage.

Gradually, a fairly functional go cart began to take shape. Although Randy and Michael still chafed a bit under their oldest brother's take-charge ways, Michael had to admit to himself that Carl Jr. was the most qualified of the lot to head up their de facto engineering department. He also recognized that "in a world of blind men, a one-eyed man was king"—a cliché which rather adequately described their collective building talents.

Their efforts were somewhat successful, but the Raptor boys' interest waned rapidly when Thad made it clear that in light of the fact that it was his welder and mostly his parts which had created the masterpiece, while the Raptors would be free to come over and use it, the go-cart would remain at his place.

The fact that the Raptors had supplied the motor and wheels and done most of the assembly, not to mention the motivation, was not enough to convince the strong-willed Swedish kid otherwise. The craft would remain at the Svensons. This new development so disheartened the Raptor boys that the go cart was never completely finished.

At the end of the second summer, Shem told Michael that he would not need him anymore but that Doug was willing to hire him the next summer. He seemed quite doubtful that it would work out, but Michael was ready to give it a try. Months later, the story got around that Shem fired him because he thought Michael had unresolved spiritual problems. This may or may not have been true, but if it was, Michael knew where it had originated.

The Clayton church was having their annual revival meetings, and a cornucopia of immorality was being confessed, especially among the young people. Immortality seemed to be somewhat of an ongoing weakness in that congregation, and one night when the Raptors visited a service, Michael's friend and Cousin Corey responded at the altar. They rode back to Corey's home on the back of a flatbed farm truck, and Michael, who was completely oblivious to the goings-on, asked Corey what it was all about.

Over the next weeks, Corey told him everything, and when the conviction gave way to the desires in the following weeks, he invited Michael to get involved. Michael was shocked to learn how pervasive the problem was. He was intrigued by the whole sex scene, but his scarred past had left him with a permanent craving for female love and relationship which was stronger than the carnal lust.

He was getting bolder and learning how to interact with girls, and if he would have had a puppy for every case of puppy love he engaged in, he could have powered several dogsleds! Puppy love was so much fun, even though he had to keep it totally hidden from his parents. The thrill of knowing that someone thought him special and wanted to be with him above all others never got old!

# SHERRI

Eventually, one girl became the focus of his undivided attentions. Her name was Sherri, and she was from the free-wheeling Bannon family, a younger sister to cousin Henry's wife. She was a fit, attractive girl with dark blonde hair. Michael, whose hair was so jet-black that it was often commented on, had always preferred black-haired girls, but there was something about Sherri that attracted him with an increasing magnetism. She was intelligent but not noticeably extroverted and seemed very comfortable with who and what she was, which Michael was definitely not!

The Bannon kids occasionally would show up at the Glendale youth activities but not often unless it was for sporting activities. Henry always liked them to be at softball and hockey games to raise the overall competency level of the players which definitely needed raising.

The disparity between Ralph and Brian Bannons' athletic skills and most of the others' in the games was glaringly obvious. While they must have been somewhat bored with so little genuine competition, they never put on airs or belittled the mistakes of their less competent teammates. Instead, they took time to help them become better players and athletes. Brian would eventually go on to become a high school coach.

The Bannon family had been through several tragedies. On one occasion, the men were target practicing with rifles when their little sister inexplicably ran across the line of fire and was fatally struck by a bullet.

Another tragedy was more prolonged. A little daughter was fighting a losing battle with leukemia for which there was very little medical help at the time. Her father was taking it very hard as he watched his daughter die by the inch. Michael heard his pastor describe how he had been at the hospital when the doctor advised him to gather the family to say their last goodbyes to her. Her father was out plowing and was near the middle of the plowed field when he saw the pastor's car, and he knew immediately what was happening. He jumped from the tractor and began running across the field of freshly plowed furrows, stumbling repeatedly in his haste. Finally, halfway across the field, he stopped, removed his cap, and sank to his knees to connect with his God, then he stood, replaced his farmer's cap, and hurried the rest of the way to the car which took him immediately to the bedside of his dying little girl. A few hours later, she passed on to be with her sister in death.

When the new school year started, Michael was shocked to see Sherri among the new students. Her family moved around a lot, and she had gone to different schools, but now they were in the same district as him. School had suddenly become a very inviting place to be, and he could envision a most enjoyable school year indeed!

Sherri wore the little white fishnet bonnet on her head that all Mennonite women and girls were required to wear and that made her different from the other girls and in junior high school. Different meant odd and odd meant unacceptable. Many decades later, the weirder a kid is, the cooler they would be esteemed to be.

But in the here and now, kids made every effort to blend in to avoid persecution from being different. There was no way for Mennonite girls to bend in with the ubiquitous white caps on their heads for which they were often scorned and ridiculed. The Raptors lived in a different school district from their church friends, so this was Michael's first exposure to what Mennonite girls had to live with. Michael was impressed with her poise and her obvious comfort "in her own skin." He was almost her magnetic opposite in his self-image. His worthlessness had been literally pounded into him for over a decade, and now he was trying to sort out the confusing dynamics of people actually liking him and respecting certain things about him.

Although they weren't in any classes together, they found opportunities to talk as the school year progressed. Michael wasn't sure why she was interested in him. People said he was a good-looking kid with his jet-black hair and brown eyes. But he tended to be a bit on the chubby side compared to his skinny brothers at times and was average at best in sports.

When he pondered these things, he often thought back to a summer night on the Big Timber reservation. They had an old army surplus tent pitched in the back yard where the boys slept sometimes. One night, Uncle Rusty was sleeping out there with the three older boys, and he began to wax eloquent about his love life.

Uncle Rusty was a movie-star-handsome, half-Chippewa Indian who had been adopted by Grandma and Grandpa Raptor when he was a baby. Now in his late teen years, he had become lover boy extraordinaire. The girls could not resist him in spite of his wild ways. Indeed, most of the type he went for loved him because of his wild ways!

That night, Rusty was telling his spellbound young nephews that if they would love any girl, she would love them back because that's how love works. Michael pondered that assertion for some time. "Are you saying that any girl you decide to love will love you back?" he finally asked.

"Yes," his uncle responded, "that's the way love works!"

"Well, if you love a princess, will she love you back?" Michael persisted.

"Sure," Rusty asserted, "she would love me if I loved her!"

Michael was still rather doubtful, but he wasn't real sure what love was, and he was still pondering the dynamics of it all when sleep had finally claimed him.

Now, at fifteen years of age, he was noticing girls and learning to interact with them. There were several cute ones in their youth group, but this Sherri was really edging the others out!

# PROJECTS

Meanwhile, the new addition on the house was coming along nicely. Carl had cut out an upstairs window to make it into a doorway, but there was a rafter board partially blocking the temporary doorway, making it necessary to duck one's head every time they walked from the old upstairs into the new. One day after months of building, Charlotte was giving several of her sisters a tour of the project. They stopped at the obstructed doorway, then Charlotte ducked under it to lead the way. Carl, who was working on the new part, instructed her sisters to wait a moment, then he fired up the chain saw and, with two quick cuts, removed the obstructing board.

Charlotte was a bit indignant. "Here I have been ducking under that board for months, then when my sisters show up you finally cut it out!" she remarked tartly.

Michael watched in disgust as Carl looked at her sisters with a cheesy grin and choked out a gurgle of something supposed to pass as laughter. "It's a good thing you came," he gurgled again, "or that board might have been there all year."

Charlotte treated him to a withering glare which Michael thought was well deserved at several levels!

Michael had become Carl's main assistant on the project now that his older brothers had real jobs. Randy had gotten a job at a Feed Mill, and Carl Jr. was working for his uncle Donald in the carpenter business. Michael established his credentials one evening when Carl was trying to wire up a new switch to the basement lights. When he had attached the wires to the light fixtures, there were two wires, white and black, to attach to the two terminals on the fixture. He then attached the two wires to the two terminals on the switch, but every time he flipped the switch, the fuse would blow.

After the destruction of about the third fuse, he gave up and asked Michael to see if he could figure it out. In spite of his total lack of experience with electrical wiring, Michael understood that electricity flows through wires like water flows through a garden hose. The switch was not to be fed with both positive and negative wires but rather to be inserted into the line to connect and interrupt the flow of electricity to the light, thereby turning it on and off as desired. He reconnected the wires, and it worked perfectly the first time. And also, for the first time in his life, Michael saw a tiny spark of respect in his father's eyes.

He laid awake in bed a long time that night thinking about the strangeness of that moment. The one thing he had never in his life experienced was any smidgen of respect from either of his parents. He had seen it bestowed on his older brothers at times. Carl Jr. had on rare occasions earned respect for his hard work and building abilities, and of course the great scholastic achievements of Randy earned him much respect, but the difficult third son really didn't seem to have anything in him worthy of his parents' respect. He had, however, found respect from other adults, especially Uncle Donald who treated him like an adult even as he mentored and taught him the building trade.

He also enjoyed respect and acceptance from many of the Glendale adults as well as the youth, which had totally transformed his life from the piece of property he had been for the first thirteen years to an actual person. He had noticed a difference in the past few transformative years in how the Glendale adults respected their youth and children compared to how the Clayton adults seemed to consider theirs as somewhat second-class citizens. In time, he came to recognize that the more conservative a church congregation is, the more they are defined and managed by top-down power structures.

The next project Carl wanted to tackle was to turn a large closet upstairs into a full bathroom but was not sure how to do the plumbing. The main problem was the need for a three-inch diameter pipe to carry the sewage from the commode. When they ripped the plaster off the walls, they discovered a three-inch vent pipe rising up through the roof to vent the commode on the main floor.

"There is our answer," Michael stated, pointing to the vent pipe.

Carl gave him a blank look. "How are we going to get the sewage in there?" he asked. "There is no connecter to tie into."

"We can cut a hole in that pipe and weld a coupling to it if we can get hold of a welder," Michael asserted. Carl looked skeptical but said he would check around for a welder to use. A few weeks later, he had a proposal for the boys. They would all pool their money, and he would pitch in the rest to buy a shiny new red Lincoln welder. The boys eagerly agreed, with thoughts of a genuine welded together go-cart in mind.

The next week, much to their excitement, Carl brought home the new welder. It had come complete with the kind of ultra-cheap welding helmet that always harvested a nice sampling of hair each time it was removed from the head. Carl managed to get the welder tapped into the fuse box, and when he flipped the switch on, it emitted a happy buzz.

Carl bought a threaded piece of pipe and, after burning a hole in the vent pipe, tried to weld the new threaded segment over the hole. Apparently, he had taken lessons from the "welder" who had built his prized pickup rack because while his welds closely resembled the globules on the rack, the new piece developed a nasty habit of falling off after he had welded it on! He finally gave up and told Michael to give it a try. While his welds were not terribly smooth, he managed to weld it in place, so it stayed on and didn't leak when water was passed through it. The taste of victory was sweet as he contemplated the many cumulative hours of relief his handiwork would provide folks in the coming years! *E=MC squared, who cared? To be able to weld a commode drain fitting—that was the thing!*

# Meeting Nathan

That summer Michael went to work for Doug and Annie Byler. At first, he found Doug a bit intimidating, but his wife Annie was just about as kind to him as any lady had ever been. Working for the hard-driving Doug was good for him, and he was actually beginning to enjoy his work. Doug would respectfully point out areas to him where he had messed up or could improve, and he tried to respond in a positive way. Michael loved pulling pranks on Annie who had a fine sense of humor.

Michael had never liked wearing a watch, so he carried a pocket watch, a fact which they were unaware of. He made Annie believe he could tell time by the sun, and she was constantly testing him. They would be in the barn milking the cows and out of the blue she would say, "What time is it right now?"

"Let me go out and check the sun," he would respond, and while he was out, he would sneak a glance at his pocket watch then come back in and report the time right to the minute. After many tests of his incredible gift, she shared it with Doug who also had to test him on it. Michael didn't want to fool Doug though, so when Doug asked him how he did it, he pulled out the pocket watch and showed it to him. Doug hooted with laughter. He especially enjoyed the fact that his wife was totally convinced that Michael could tell time to the minute by the position of the sun!

Often on beautiful summer evenings, Doug would position a large box type silage wagon at the edge of the field behind the house for a backstop and lay out plates of plywood for bases then invite the church folks or family over for a softball game. In this way, Michael got better acquainted with his many cousins from the Clayton church.

The Clayton church demanded a much stricter dress code than he was used to, and he wondered why that was so important to them. They seemed to be constantly riding their young people about everything from the guys' hair length and type of shirts and trousers to the girls' hairstyles or dress designs. They had very detailed and specific requirements as to how the white caps they wore must be made, how they were to make their dresses, and what type of hosiery was acceptable.

All the girls and women's dresses were handmade because the required designs could not be bought commercially. They were to be well below the knee in length and must have an extra layer of loose-fitting cloth covering the bosom to hide any feminine shape. There were many other specific rules governing nearly every aspect of their lives.

Michael was not a total stranger to church related regulations, but he was not used to them playing so great a part in the members' everyday lives. He didn't dwell on it much though because hyper-control was all their family had ever known, and he was more apt to notice the little bits of freedom they were beginning to see in this new world. As he got older, this would all play a greater role in his daily existence.

One day, he was riding with Doug in his ancient pickup back from his second farm when they met Doug's brother-in-law Art coming in the long dirt lane. Doug stopped to chat with Art, and Michael noticed a somewhat scrawny kid riding along in Art's truck. He seemed rather small with blond hair, and he was very friendly and outgoing. He smiled at Michael and called over a cheerful "Hi there!" Michael returned the greeting, but he wasn't good at striking up new friendships, so his response was rather stilted. He couldn't possibly know at this point that the blond kid would in time become one of his best friends ever and influence his life tremendously!

When the conversation ended and they were again bouncing down the rutted dirt lane, Michael's thoughts remained on the gregarious little blond kid with the friendly smile. "Who was that little kid with Art?" he asked Doug.

Doug levelled a slow, speculative look at his hired helper, then responded, "That boy is Nathan Friedman from the settlement up at Birchwood."

"You know," he added dryly, "you aren't all that big yourself!"

*Well, at least he didn't use tired old fat accusation,* Michael thought philosophically. *I guess all that meanness comes from my family members.*

Hay making season was always a big part of every summer. It was hot and scratchy work, but there was something enjoyable about it. Michael had gotten used to Shem's new bale throwing baler, and it was a step back to have to have someone riding on the flatbed hay wagon and stack the bales manually as they pushed their way out the back of the baler.

Stacking bales on the wagon behind the baler was often very hot with the afternoon sun blazing down on you as the tractor and baler thump thumped its way around the field gobbling up the serpentine row of dried hay. When the hay was thick, the wagon stacker was kept hustling to grab the rectangular bales by the strings and swing them up on the growing stack on the trailer.

At times, however, the hay rows would be thinner, and the job could be much easier. The baler compressed the hay into bales by means of a piston driven ram which made a loud continuous *thump, thump, thump*ing. This loud thumping added to the dull roar of the tractor engine on a warm sunny afternoon could be almost hypnotic if one wasn't scrambling to keep up with the bales popping out the chute from the baler.

The toughest job by far was stacking hay in the haymow of the barn. Most barns were constructed with a large upper story, often with a hip roofed design to accommodate more hay storage. The temperature in the mow on a hot summer day reached well over a hundred degrees.

There was very little air movement, and the air was often filthy from the bales falling from the hay elevator and dropping to the barn floor where they would land with a bounce which created a small shower of hay dust. The strongest and toughest men usually handled this awful job, and they needed to keep a supply of drinking water within easy reach at all times. They would emerge afterward covered with hay dust, soaked with sweat, with faces flushed from the ordeal.

One of Michael's older cousins, Paul Manning, was married and lived on an old farm directly across the road from the Byler farm. Doug stored hay in the haymow of his barn. One day, Doug sent Michael over to unload a hay wagon. Paul helped Michael unload the wagon, then when they were finished, Paul's wife appeared with ice cold lemonade, and they sat down in the barn to enjoy it. As they sipped the lemonade, they became so engrossed in conversation that Michael totally lost track of the time. Farmers only had so many wagons to work with, and the unspoken sin was for the person unloading not to keep an empty wagon available at all times so the all-important baler can keep baling. Doug had loaded two wagons and was becoming very frustrated at the delay.

Michael and Paul were deep in conversation when Doug came blasting through the barn door and saw them chatting and enjoying the lemonade. Michael recognized the hot anger in his eyes; he had seen it all his life in his father. He had, however, never seen a man manage his anger in such a self-controlled manner. Doug did issue a stern rebuke, but it was done decently without the accordant profanity Michael had so often heard. He would never forget this—the first time he had ever seen intense anger properly managed by self-control.

# UNREPENTANT COWS
# AND A KISS

While Michael enjoyed farm life, he had never really liked cows. In his mind cows were useful only for herding from horseback or roping and branding. The whole process of crawling under cows to extract their milk was just not cool! Most farms had their cows tied in long rows with a manger at their heads and a gutter behind their back legs to collect their droppings and squirtings. When the cows would lay down to sleep, their tails would get a good soaking in the gutter and the little tuft of hair at the end would get thoroughly soaked with a mix of cow manure and urine.

Cows are not known as aggressive animals, and unless they have horns, they are without offensive weapons. But they did have unpleasant things in store for the unfortunate farming folks who got into their space to extract their milk. Chief among their limited defensive arsenal was their ability to deliver vicious forward kicks with their back legs. Often these kicks incorporated a somewhat circular outward swing to include the area where the hapless farmer was now squatting. Some of them could deliver kicks with power and lightning speed and many a farmer was sent sprawling, and some even ended up at the doctor or chiropractor's office.

Michael had witnessed cows send farmers flying from these kicks, and on some occasions, he actually saw the cow turn her head and look directly at her hurting victim. While she couldn't verbalize her irritations, the message in her eyes was clear: *there's lots more where that came from, buddy!*

The real messy form of cow vengeance though, came from well-placed smacks of her gutter-soaked tail. Michael thought the cows might have had contests among themselves for marksmanship because the level of accuracy seemed to improve with time and practice. Getting whacked by the solid part of the tail could hurt, but there was no substitute for the sheer beauty of scoring a bullseye hit across the face with the saturated tuft of hair at the end of her tail. At these times, not only would the cow look around to check her accuracy, Michael thought he might have even seen some of them grin with satisfaction! Some farmers would cut the tails off their cows to avoid just this sort of bovine vengeance, but cows have tails for reasons other than whacking unsuspecting farmers, and a cow with no tail was defenseless against flies in the summer.

While Michael's disgust for these animals grew as the years passed, far away in another state, a young Mennonite girl his age was holding outdoor services with them. Her father was a preacher, and on lazy summer afternoons, she would shanghai whomever she could of her brothers or sisters and press them into service ministering to the cows. Services included singing, praying, and preaching. Invitations to the alter were not included because none of the cows ever repented of their sins. This little black-haired girl with pigtails would one day become Michael's wife. They would forever disagree about cows!

That summer would be Michael's last working for Doug. He had learned much and grown a few more inches. He had always been just a bit short compared to his older brothers, and even Johnny was showing a possibility of catching him in height. Carl Jr. was so tall for his age that he had to endure an unending parade of tall jokes such as "How's the weather up there?"

Randy could always be depended upon to keep Michael humble about his lack of height. It was with his height as it was with his weight. He was not short or fat for his age, but compared to his tall skinny brothers, he came up short.

Charlotte loved to line all five sons up by age and take their picture. For years, it was a pretty even stair step layout except Michael's step was a bit lower than it should have been for good symmetry. He suffered no end of persecution from Randy about this for years until he got a late growth spurt and became the second tallest of the five sons. When that happened, Randy was all done making an issue of height, and he can be seen in subsequent photos obviously straining for height because the dip was now on his step. His mother obligingly stopped taking the age lineup photos. It was okay for Michael to look odd in pictures, but now that Randy was showing the short dip, well…she actually had enough stair-step lineup pictures!

Much to Michael's delight, the Bannons had moved to a house close to the Glendale church and would occasionally come to their church. Somewhere deep in his darker self, a plan was beginning to take shape.

Doug owned a second farm about a mile across the highway from his home farm, and he often left his ancient Chevy pickup there with the key in the ignition. Michael had no driver's license, but he occasionally drove the pickup around the farm for various projects.

He was spending more time with his cousin Corey, and they had talked of sneaking out and doing something together some night. Corey took the same risks as Michael if they got caught. His father also had a wild temper and once beat Corey's back into a bloody pulp.

The plan was for Corey to sneak out of his house and push his small motorcycle down the lane then ride it over to meet Michael at the second farm where the ancient pickup waited to take him courting. Michael made sure there was plenty of gas in the truck. What could possibly go wrong?

That night, he went to bed with his clothes on and waited until he was sure everyone was asleep. He had to sneak down the bare wooden stairs and out the door without making a sound, then run the mile to where the truck was parked. By some miracle, he made it. But there was no sign of Corey.

He waited for nearly an hour then decided to go on alone. He started the truck and was about halfway out the lane when a dark-clad figure leaped from the bushes into the road. It was Corey. He had had to wait extra-long for the family to settle down and fall asleep, then the motorcycle had not wanted to cooperate, but he had made it. They headed out on the fifteen-mile journey to the Bannons, passing through one small village on their way. Michael drove as fast as he dared. He had told Sherri he would be coming and at what time she could expect him. He was pretty sure she didn't believe him, which made it extra important that he show.

A light drizzle was falling when they finally pulled into the Bannons' driveway. There was a light on above the front step, and Michael knocked on the door as Sherri had told him to do. That had been the subject of much discussion between them. Michael had said, "What if your dad comes to the door?" and she had responded, "He probably will, why would that matter?" He could totally not conceive of any father allowing his daughter to spend time with a boyfriend in a truck in the middle of the night!

But she had insisted that it was not a problem, so he complied. Sure enough, the door was opened by Mr. Bannon himself who promptly offered to go fetch his daughter. Her older sister came with her and slid in in on the bench seat beside Corey, while Sherri snuggled in beside Michael.

"I can't believe you came," she murmured.

"Yup," he said, "I told you I was gonna come over tonight."

He put his arm around her, and she snuggled even closer. Michael was way out of his comfort zone and trying hard not to show it. He had never been the least bit physical with a girl except to hold hands on a few occasions. They completely lost track of time as they talked, hugged, and held hands. He was trying to get up the nerve to kiss her, but he had never kissed a girl before, and the only thing he knew about kissing was the perfunctory pecks he had seen others exchange.

There was nothing sexual about their time together that night, but it would remain one of and perhaps *the* most special night of his entire life! He finally decided to go for the kiss. Although they were sitting beside each other, she was partway on his lap, and they were turned toward each other. Michael began the proverbial lean in, and she met him halfway. He kissed her full on the mouth and then leaned back out partway. He didn't know what kind of response to expect, but what came next blew all his circuits! Smiling her smile that made him feel all squishy inside, she slowly reached out her left hand and cupped his chin. Then with her other hand behind his head, she slowly drew him back in for a real kiss.

Michael never knew what hit him! When their mouths met again, and she began demonstrating how kissing is really done, little Michael suddenly became *big, bad Mike*! Feelings and emotions were exploding inside him that he never knew existed! An incredible boldness and sense of raw electricity surged through him like never before, much of which would never leave him.

But the clock was spinning wildly, and they needed to leave. He finally mustered enough self-control to walk the girls back to their door and bid them goodnight. He wasn't sure if he walked or floated back to the pickup for the trip back to the farm. The night had been perfect—so far.

They were about a mile down the road when the first sign of trouble appeared. He noticed the headlights were barely putting out any light and the windshield wipers had ceased their anemic strokes altogether. Doug had not informed him that the charging system was not working on this pickup, and thus far it had been drawing power from a single six-volt battery which was now dead. The truck soon died completely, and they coasted to a stop beside the road. They were in a very serious predicament, but Michael was still euphoric. He almost felt like he could tuck the pickup under his arm and carry it home.

But the high finally ebbed, and they discussed their very limited options. The Stevens lived a few miles down the road and Leighton had just gotten his own car and while they knew he would be willing to tow them back, they didn't know how to wake him without his parents finding out. They finally decided they would have to just knock on the door and play it out as it came. Corey knocked on the door while Michael waited in the shadows. Mike answered the door, and after a bit of grilling, he went and got Leighton to come and help them.

Leighton was highly animated by the whole crazy romantic venture, and he produced a chain from the shed and was soon towing them back to the farm. The escapade created a close bond between him and Michael that would last for years. When Leighton's father interrogated him about it the next morning, he begged and cajoled him into keeping the secret. Neither of them would ever know what severe beatings their silence saved Michael and Corey from receiving for their fiasco.

The next day, Doug saw that his truck had been messed with, since it was parked differently, and the battery was completely dead. Michael knew he had to confess his malfeasance to him before the summer was over, but he kept putting it off, and it got harder to do.

Finally one night as he lay on his bed upstairs, the guilt became more than he could stand. He lay there praying for courage to go down and make the confession and suddenly felt a strange power help lift him off the bed and almost run down the stairs.

Doug was still up, and Michael made his confession to him. He only confessed the part about using his truck, he didn't give details of where he had gone and who was involved. Doug seemed a bit blown away but freely forgave him and the matter was laid to rest.

Michael often marveled that Mike Stevens had kept his secret. Many decades later, he would encounter Mike at a social event, and Mike looked at him strangely and cracked, "You still owe me about a thousand dollars for keeping your secret!" If he had been serious, Michael would have been willing to pay him on the spot.

The night of the kiss awakened something in Michael that had been sorely needed. He was still dealing with his chronic fear, but now he had learned that he had the courage to take risks for things that were important to him. And while he still enjoyed other girls, only Sherri held his heart. He would have done anything for her. In time, his mother caught wind of his interest in her and waged a full-scale effort to keep them apart. But she couldn't monitor his actions at school, so the relationship continued.

Michael couldn't understand his mother's hatred for the relationship. Sherri was not known as a bad girl in any way, so he figured it just must because of her intense dislike of him. Years later, he would discover that at one time in her youth, she had had a relationship going with Larry Bannon, and he had ended the relationship. Typical of her nature, she began to despise him and could never again say one nice thing about him or his family. It was not difficult for her to manipulate her husband into seeing them her way as well.

# THE GUITAR

Milford Eberly was member of the Glendale church who owned a small farm on the outskirts of the community. He also did some auto repair work including body repair. He was the "go-to" person for most of the Mennonites who needed their cars of pickups worked on because his rates were far cheaper than the repair shops in town.

The Eberly family was fairly large. Michael always found visits there interesting because of the large scope of things Milford had going on. He seemed to be fairly good at whatever he did, but at the same time, excelled at nothing he did. His farm was littered with a mixture of farm equipment, cow manure, cars, and trucks awaiting repair, with assorted parts scattered everywhere.

His numerous children were for the most part well behaved and taught to work alongside their parents. The oldest girl was rather small and mild mannered, and people teased Carl Jr. about her being his girlfriend. They had no interest in each other, it just tickled the imaginations of some of the more easy-to-amuse individuals to think of them as a couple—him tall, gangly, and more outgoing with her small, compact, and quiet. Their teasing irritated Carl Jr. which, of course, encouraged more of the same.

But it was her younger brother Abner who garnered the most attention. There was nothing reserved about him. He was fairly good-looking with dark hair and eyes, and he loved to drive the various cars available through his father's repair business. In addition to repairing customers' vehicles, Milford would purchase wrecked vehicles and repair them to sell at a profit.

Several of the Glendale people had bought repaired vehicles from him including Leon Kurtz's younger brother Danny. The car

Danny had bought was a sporty-looking fastback that gleamed with a new paint job. It seemed to drive well, but folks following it noticed that it dog-tracked severely. Where a normal car will only leave two tire trails in the snow, this car left four. But it seemed to get its occupants from point A to point B, so down the road it cruised!

One Sunday, the Raptors were invited to the Eberlys for dinner after the morning church service. After the meal, Milford took the guys out to show them his auto repair shop. His main repair project was a 1966 Chevelle Malibu, and the boys were very impressed with the sleek, sporty design of the car. The right front fender had been damaged in a minor accident, and Milford was building it back into shape with layers of Bondo body filler. They had never seen Bondo before, so he explained how it works then demonstrated its durability by rapping smartly on the repaired surface with a hammer.

Carl Jr. was very taken with the car, and Milford told him that he planned to sell it as soon as it was repaired. Carl Jr. began making arrangements to buy it with the money he would get from selling the Fairlane and money he had earned. The car turned out to be a sound investment and stayed in the family for years, even after Carl Jr. moved on to a brand new car in Pennsylvania.

Abner became known for his vigorous testing of the various cars' capabilities, and he was not afraid of being labelled boastful. In time, the Glendale youth guys assigned him the affectionate name "Evil Abner" for his automotive exploits.

Michael was several years younger than Evil Abner, so he didn't know him well. He had heard the stories of his wild driving and thought he must be an interesting fellow. He had also heard some of his boasting and thought the guy really should tone it down a bit. He could see it turned some of the girls off as well as the guys, but then everybody had their down sides.

One Sunday, Charlotte invited the Eberly family to Sunday dinner after the church service. It was very common among Mennonites to invite another family to their homes for dinner after the morning service. It was a logical time to socialize since any type of work that was not absolutely essential (such as feeding livestock or milking cows) was strictly forbidden.

The Ten Commandments strictly forbade working on the Sabbath, and the first incidence of capital punishment in the new nation of Israel after God gave them their long list of rules occurred in the fifteenth chapter of the book of Numbers when a man was stoned to death for gathering sticks to make a fire on the sabbath.

Even though the Bible goes on in the New Testament to explain in painstaking detail how the one enormous sacrifice, the Son of God himself, was made to end all the animal sacrifices with their attendant rules, many religions still held to a critical need to keep certain parts of the old Jewish law and attach sinful connotations to those who didn't

From the earliest Christians, contemporaries of Jesus himself, to modern-day believers, it would be tremendously difficult to grasp the fact that this great sacrifice ushered in an entire new premise where salvation comes by grace through faith and that alone. The intense need within people to contribute something to this grace to help them qualify for salvation has been a lethal snare from day one. The snare of that need is that grace stands alone, and if something is added to it, it disappears. When it disappears, the only recourse for a religious group is to live by rules and regulations to effect the appearance of the same outcome. Hence, the critical importance of rules in maintaining religious organizations.

The underlying irony of the whole concept of keeping the Sabbath, however, centered around a fact that astonishingly few Christian professing people knew. The Sabbath is Saturday—*not* Sunday as so many assume it to be. If there is a legalistic need to "keep the Sabbath," the Seventh Day Adventists are the ones who get it right. Most Christian groups observe Sunday as the "Lord's day" because it is fairly plain in the New Testament that the Early Church observed the "first day of the week" as their holy day.

The day the Eberlys came for Sunday dinner, Michael's life would again be impacted forever. And it would come about by a little help from Evil Abner.

After the meal, the guys were hanging around in the guys' bedroom when Abner spotted Michael's cheap guitar propped up in the corner. "Who plays the guitar?" he asked, picking it up and examining it.

"It's mine," Michael answered, "and I can't learn how to play it!"

Abner shot a puzzled glance at him. "Why not?" he asked. "It's not that hard to play guitar."

"Well, it's impossible for me!" Michael shot back, angry frustration tingeing his voice. "I have been trying my best for years, and I just can't get it!" He suspected Abner was putting on a boastful bluff. He had never seen a guitar in his hand when the Glendale youth made music. But he was in for a shock!

Abner was twisting the string tensioners and plucking the strings to test the tuning like someone who knew what he was doing. "Do you know how to play it?" Michael asked, the disbelief obvious in his voice.

"Sure," Abner replied. "It's easy if you can sing. You can sing, can't you?"

"Sure," Michael responded, "but what does that have to do with playing guitar?"

By now, Abner was strumming the guitar. "Watch," he instructed. "I'll show you. You only need to know three chords to get you started. Here are the three I started with." He proceeded to show Michael how to place his fingers for the keys of G, C, and D7. Then he slowly began to sing a familiar song displaying the changes in finger positions to synchronize the guitar music with his voice.

Michael was astounded! *After all these years of painfully desperate effort, could it really be this simple?*

Abner showed him again how to hold the chords then change between them as the song required. Then he handed the instrument to Michael and helped him place his fingers correctly.

Miracle of miracles! It really wasn't that impossible! As his fingers became more familiar with the chord placings, he slowly began to make the guitar's music match that of his voice. His song was slow, and there were many discordant contributions from the guitar, but *he was finally playing guitar!*

In the following weeks, Michael's playing improved dramatically. He would always be grateful to his parents for buying him that first guitar. And he would always be especially grateful to "Evil Abner" for teaching him how to make it sing for him! He would never achieve the competency of the Kurtz family, but his guitar playing would play a significant role in the rest of his life.

# PANCAKE EATING CONTEST

Because the Raptor kids were closely related to so many of the Clayton young people, they would occasionally be invited to Clayton youth's social functions. One evening they were invited to the home of Uncle Gary and Aunt Paula Manning for a pancake eating contest. Aunt Paula was very close to her sister Charlotte Raptor, so their families often got together for picnics and outings. Uncle Gary was a robust, likeable man whose laid-back personality earned him the status of hen-pecked husband. He was quite popular with the Reynolds boys though, in part because he faithfully took them hunting and taught them how to shoot.

The Mannings were a farm family, and Uncle Gary supplemented his farm income with a business whitewashing the interiors of barns. He was rather careless about his personal safety and as a result often got his eyes burned from the lime base of the whitewash.

In spite of his damaged eyes, Uncle Gary was an incredibly good marksman. He took time to help his young nephews adjust the sights of their rifles to achieve perfect aim. He had several interesting rifles, one of which was a very antiquated .22 caliber bolt action which he loaned to Michael.

Michael was so impressed with it that Uncle Gary offered to sell it to him for twelve dollars—an offer which was immediately snapped up by Michael. He refinished the stock and took loving care of the old gun until the day he passed it on to his son.

The evening of the pancake eating contest, the Mannings had set up tables and chairs in the dining room and living room. There were extra burners set up in the kitchen where some of the youth girls would help Aunt Paula crank out the pancakes. Everyone knew that the contest would be between the boys, and Michael was pretty sure that his brother Randy would win.

Randy was as thin as a stick but was known in the Raptor household for his voracious appetite. His mother often claimed that when she cooked chicken for supper, she needed to cook two chickens; one for the family and one for Randy. This claim sometimes irritated Randy, but it was not far from being accurate!

As the eating competition began, huge stacks of pancakes were delivered to the tables which disappeared like magic into the hungry stomachs of young people, many of whom had not eaten all day just for this occasion. The girls soon began to drop out of the eating and were content to watch the rest of the competitors.

One by one, the boys dropped out, and finally, the competition was down to two of the older boys. Michael was rather proud of the fact that Randy was still going strong. His only remaining competitor was his cousin, David Wenger. David was the son of Charlotte's oldest sister, Anita, who had married a stern rather quiet, God-fearing man named Neil Wenger. Together they had raised a large family of sons and daughters.

Neil was the bishop of the Clayton church, and he ruled it with an iron fist. Their family was for the most part talented and intelligent, and many of the sons would in time be ordained to ministry.

By now, the avalanche of pancakes from the kitchen had slowed to a trickle, and everyone was gathered around the dining room table to see who would win this contest of abject gluttony. Randy had a rather significant advantage in that in lieu of syrup, his cousin had eaten all of his with chocolate pudding.

The rather questionable honor of winning the contest was the only thing keeping the contest alive now. One young man would eat a pancake, putting him in the lead, and then the other would follow suit. They finally agreed to call it a draw, but the conscientious Randy always pointed out that his cousin was really the winner because of all the pudding topping he had consumed with his pancakes. Between them, they had consumed thirty-eight thick pancakes about six inches in diameter!

# BUGGY-BORNE BRETHREN

Grandpa Raptors were coming to visit. The Raptor boys were excited to see them again and didn't mind when their mother predictably pressed them into service getting the house and lawn all cleaned up. Grandpa and Grandma Raptor were very much loved by their Ohio grandchildren. They had stayed behind in South Dakota for a few more years after Carl's family had move to Ohio. Finally, they had sold their farm and prepared to move to Pennsylvania where their son John lived with his family. They had sold everything in South Dakota except for a piece of land with a gravel pit on it. Grandpa received small monthly checks from the county for the gravel they took from his pit and did not want to sell it. Grandma was pretty sure the county was "ripping him off," but easygoing Grandpa just kept cashing the little checks and calling it all profit.

While digging the gravel out, the excavators had unearthed a huge boulder which they had pushed up to the side of the road with their bulldozer. Someone had painted neatly on the boulder "*Jesus saves*" as a testimony to the unsaved folks in the county. Much to Grandma's irritation, some anonymous ne'er-do-well had sneaked in and added some supplementary text. The boulder now read: *Jesus saves gold bond stamps!*

Grandma and Grandpa finally arrived with their car packed out to the max and towing an equally packed trailer. They were swarmed by their adoring grandkids and said they planned to stay for a few days before moving on to Pennsylvania.

In the course of their visit, they invited Carl Jr. to come out east with them. The house they were renting had plenty of room, and they were sure Uncle John could get him a job with the construction company he worked for. By some miracle of destiny, Carl and Charlotte agreed.

Carl Jr. had been working for his uncle Donald Reynolds, and they seemed to get along well. But opportunities to escape the dictatorial Raptor household were nearly nonexistent, and he seized the opportunity. He was nineteen now, tall for his age, and had accumulated a fair amount of experience in the home construction business. While Michael was sad to see him go, he was very happy for his brother's sake that he could now actually begin to live his own life.

Several days later, Carl Jr. and his most needed possessions were packed in with Grandpa's load, and they were headed out the driveway to a new world and a new life. He had been instructed by his parents to send a percentage of his income home to them. They had always taken a chunk of their sons' earnings which seemed reasonable as long as they were providing food and lodging for them. But Michael wondered how Carl Jr. would have enough to pay Grandpas for food and lodging besides his everyday expenses if he still had to send money back home. It seemed like a rip-off to him, but he recognized that he didn't have a dog in that hunt, so he said nothing about it. The beatings had mostly tapered off to fairly frequent blows to the face or kicks to the rear, and he tried to be careful not to upset the new status quo.

Some weeks later when Carl Jr. had landed a job with Uncle John's boss, Carl and Charlotte travelled out to visit him and Grandpa in their new home. Carl Jr would never move out of his newly adopted state.

True to his word, Uncle John helped Carl Jr. hire on with his company where he thrived and enjoyed the work. He badly needed his car for work though, so Charlotte hatched a plan to bring it out to them. She and Carl would drive the car out to Pennsylvania then bring a greyhound bus home. Michael, Johnny, and Eli would go along, and Michael invited Leighton to go with them. He readily accepted the invitation. Some days later, the family was headed east in the Malibu. They packed light, knowing that they would be carrying their baggage back on the bus. Michael thought the bus trip sounded like fun, but he couldn't know that that would be the least of the adventures they would experience on the trip.

Charlotte and Carl had decided to stop along the way and visit overnight with Carl's uncle Ty and his family. Ty was a prosperous farmer who lived very close to the interstate they would be taking, and they were happy to have the Raptors stop in for the night. While the Raptor boys knew their mother's relatives quite well, they were barely acquainted with their father's. This was due in part to the big "skeleton in the closet" about the circumstances leading to his illegitimate birth. It would take years for the facts to come out in bits, pieces, and snippets to where the truth would be known to Carl's sons. When it was all sorted out, some of them were frustrated to discover that their good friends, the Masons, from their reservation days were actually their cousins. The relational coolness of their parents toward the Masons had been due to their attempt to hide the relationship and make sure no romantic situations developed between the children. In retrospect, these efforts all seemed so unnecessary and even dishonest to Michael, but he also realized that back in that day, that was how things were usually done.

They arrived at Carl's uncle Ty's farm about dusk. Ty was one of Grandma Raptor's brothers, a friendly and unassuming man, who showed them around his neat and tidy farm. Michael could see that his father was impressed with the well-maintained, modern farm machinery kept stored in large, well-kept buildings. The farm house was a modern ranch-style house with a large porch, surrounded by lush green lawns. There were beautiful flower beds and a large garden with not a weed to be seen. Ty's wife Marta served them a delicious supper during which Michael and Leighton got acquainted with their son Dana, who was just a few months older than Michael.

When the dishes were cleared away after the meal, and the adults were sitting around the living room chatting, it didn't take the gregarious Leighton long to get an interesting conversation going with Dana.

"Hey guys," Dana suggested with a gleam in his eye, "how about a cruise around the community so see some of the Amish farms?" The idea was an instant hit with the visiting boys, and Michael was amazed at how readily Dana's father handed over the keys to the family car. Only Dana had any idea how intense this drive would become!

They cruised around the county, viewing the impeccably manicured Amish farms and homesteads until dusk turned into full dark. Finally, Dana found what he had been looking for. It was an Amish farm where the lawn around the house was parked full of buggies. "It's an Amish youth singing," Dana explained, "and we are gonna keep an eye on it until the Amish Romeos start taking their girls home in their buggies."

They continued to cruise for another hour or so, stopping at a drive-in root beer stand where about a dozen souped-up muscle cars were parked. "Those cars belong to the young Amish guys who are doing their wild years," Dana explained. "When Amish boys turn sixteen, they ignore the rules of the Amish church for a few years and get their driver's licenses and buy a muscle car. They usually soup up the engines for maximum power and trick out the bodies with chrome wheels, pin striping, and all kinds of snazzy stuff. Then they run around wild for the next few years with most of them getting involved in drinking, drugs, and free sex. They tend to be pretty tough guys from their rugged upbringing on Amish farms, and it is a good idea not to tangle with them. When they get serious about marriage, they will sell their car, grow a beard, and join the Amish church, where none of their fiascos or legal troubles from their wild years will be held against them."

They left the root beer stand and cruised past the Amish singing again. There was a trickle of buggies beginning to leave, and Dana began to follow one very closely. After a few miles and several turns, the driver of the buggy became obviously spooked by the large car following so closely. "These guys are taking their girlfriends home, Dana explained, and I get a kick out of spooking them in front of their girlfriends."

A few miles later, the nervous driver whipped the buggy horse into a full run. But he was no match for the car shadowing the buggy. They were following the buggy at a distance of approximately thirty feet and matching it turn for turn. Finally, the freaked-out driver turned into the driveway of an Amish farm.

"That isn't where he was headed," Dana said, laughing. "he's just trying to shake us off."

They cruised past and went around the county block, and sure enough, when they drove back past the farm, the buggy was gone. They picked it up about a mile down the road and began following it again, just to show the driver they had not been fooled.

"Now let's go hassle someone else." Dana laughed. They cruised around again until they located another buggy and followed it like they had done the first buggy. This driver also got creeped out and began trying to evade them but to no avail. By the third or fourth buggy, the pursuers in the car were having the time of their lives! But the tables were about to get turned. Someone had gotten word to the wild Amish kids at the root beer stand that a car was hassling their brethren in buggies.

"Oh, oh," Dana said, "we've got trouble coming." Michael turned around to see a hopped up Chevelle he had noticed at the root beer stand come roaring up behind them, and with its headlights on bright, it began to follow them even closer than they were following the buggy. "We'd better knock it off," Dana remarked. "We don't want to tangle with those guys."

Another muscle car was fast approaching from the rear as Dana passed the buggy and floored the sedan. The muscle cars kept tight on his tail as he reached speeds over ninety miles per hour. The hunters were now the hunted, and while the excitement was just as high, it was not nearly as much fun now!

There was no way the family sedan could lose the souped-up muscle cars, so Dana began trying some evasive turns and maneuvers. "We don't dare let these guys box us in and stop us," he said, worry obvious in his voice.

"If they get their hands on us, they will beat the crap out of us!" Michael, who knew all about getting the crap beat out of him, felt a cold twinge of fear!

"I have one trick left," Dana said as he pulled a hard, squealing right turn onto a gravel road. The sedan fishtailed wildly for a few seconds, then the tires gained purchase on the gravel, and the big car shot forward, raising a huge cloud of dust and flying stones behind. The pursuers were not willing to push their gleaming, souped-up cars through this cloud and dropped the pursuit. Dana made a few more turns onto gravel roads then headed for home.

"I think we are okay now," Dana said, "as long as nobody called the cops."

Michael didn't feel completely safe until Dana had pulled the car into Uncle Ty's garage and closed the overhead door. Then they all had a good laugh. "That was the most fun I've had in a long time!" Leighton said, to which Michael enthusiastically agreed.

Dana just grinned at them. "Sometimes you just gotta make your own fun around here," he commented with a conspiratorial grin.

# SELLING FLICKA

Between his summer jobs and youth activities, Michael was spending less and less time at home. He rarely had time for horseback riding, and his sweet-tempered filly Flicka was getting very little attention. He sometimes found her out in the pasture and loved on her a while, then climbed on her without a saddle or bridle and guided her with the pressure of his hands and knees. He had noticed the twelve-year-old neighbor girl would do the same at times. It was like riding a big, friendly dog. Michael decided to sell her and let someone enjoy her who had more time for her. He had built a light sulky cart out of some bicycle tires and lightweight steel and taught her to pull it. The sulky seated only two, but it was much lighter than the clumsy cart Carl had built which had afforded them so much enjoyment over the years. He had also sorted through the piles of harness scraps his father kept in the barn and riveted together a lightweight racing harness to go with the sulky instead of the regular draft harness with its heavy collars and straps hanging all over the horse.

An advertisement in the local paper only cost him a few dollars, but in the busyness of the coming days, he forgot all about it. One evening near the end of the week, he received a call from his very upset mother. "Your dad says that ad you have in the paper is not true!" she barked. "It says she is gentle and well trained and some people came to look at her and he tried to ride her and she was a mess! She even tried to buck him off!"

Michael was shocked! His Flicka had never bucked in her life! He didn't think she even knew how. "Well, I'll check her out when I get home," he said lamely. He pondered the situation as he lay in bed that night. *What had come over his sweet filly to make her act that way? Maybe she was sick?*

When Michael returned home that weekend, he went directly to the pasture to check on his filly. To his relief, she seemed to be healthy and acting normal. With some trepidation, he slipped onto her back and rode her back to the barn. Nothing seemed to be wrong with her. Then Carl came walking around the corner of the barn, and Michael felt the slightest tremor run through the young horse. He instantly understood what had gone wrong. His father's abrupt appearance had had that same effect on him for years!

"I don't know, Dad," he said. "She seems to be acting normal now!"

Carl grunted an unintelligible response and kept walking. Michael slid off the filly's back and cradled her soft nose in his arms. In his mind's eye, he could see exactly what had happened. His father's method of breaking horses was through brute force until mastery and submission was achieved. It was the way horses were trained in those days. Carl was a powerful man, and horses learned to accept his mastery or suffer the consequences until they did. They learned to be led by being tied to a wagon and dragged until they cooperated.

But Carl had never had any interaction with Flicka, and Michael had trained her with gentleness and rewards for good behavior. She didn't know what it was to be kicked and slapped around, and the first thing Carl usually did after mounting a horse was to give it a slap across the ribs "to get its attention." The gentle filly had panicked from that first slap, and the more she jumped and tried to get away from him, the more the big man astride her put the boots to her. It took no imagination for Michael to realize the terror the young horse had felt. He had been there himself countless times.

That night over supper, Michael assured his parents that he would make himself available to represent the filly to future potential buyers. He and Carl were both there when a kind man came to buy her for his daughter. Much to Carl's irritation, the man was as impressed with Michael as he was the horse and said so in those words. Carl looked mightily irritated when the man commented that he sure wishes he could buy the boy with the horse! For his part, Michael was happy to know that his Flicka was going to a good home.

# THE FEED MILL
# AND A FURNACE

Life was a bit strange for the first while after Carl Jr. left. Michael had never been real close to him, mostly because of the age difference and his authoritarian way of interacting with his younger siblings, but he did respect him in a lot of ways and sensed much of the pain he lived with.

Randy was now the oldest son at home. He was working at a feed mill in the village of Conway, about ten miles from home. His older cousin Paul Manning had worked there for years and was the de facto foreman. He had gotten Randy hired, and for the most part, they got along well. Paul had a dynamic personality and enjoyed pulling informed out of his rather naïve younger cousin.

As the months passed, Randy learned how to mix livestock feeds from the various ingredient bins then mix them and unload the mixer into hundred-pound burlap sacks. There was a pile of baler twine strings cut to approximately twelve-inch lengths which were used to tie the mouth of the sacks shut, using a special knot called a miller's knot.

The full sack of feed would then be picked up and tossed onto the bed of the delivery truck. After the truck was loaded, it would be driven to the farm where it had been ordered. Many of the farms had special rooms in the barn where the cow feed was stored, and some of them were far enough from the entrance door that the one-hundred-pound sacks of feed needed to be carried from the delivery truck across the barn to the feed room.

The first few trips to the feed room would invariably disrupt the festivities of the furry rodents that made their home there. With a perpetual banquet available, it was nearly impossible to keep the mice and rats away no matter how much poison was set out for them, so they were permanent residents in the feed room.

All this heavy lifting had the happy side effect of creating hard, bulging muscles on the young men who worked there. Randy had always been quite skinny, but his chest, neck, and arms thickened noticeably. He was looking good—a fact not lost on himself or the young Miss Rene Miller.

Randy's relationship with Rene was becoming rock solid. Michael never felt any attraction to Rene, but he could easily understand why Randy was taken with her. He did feel a bit used, however, that Randy would always manipulate him and Rene's sister Bertha to accompany them to youth activities because he was not yet old enough to officially date. Bertha was a very nice girl who like Michael struggled with the weight issues, and the Raptors would constantly make jokes about what a great couple they made, even though they knew the only sparks in the foursome were between the two spending quality time together in the front seat.

Randy had recently bought his first car and Michael was very impressed with it. It was a 1967 Oldsmobile 442—a sports model two-door hardtop with a powerful four hundred cubic engine and four speed transmission. The car's power was impressive, as was its thirst for gasoline. Gas was selling for less than fifty cents a gallon, but in time, Randy got very tired of constantly refueling the beast. Still, Rene liked the car, and it was worth a lot to impress her.

The new addition to the house was nearing completion, but there was one big remaining project. The old house had no furnace, and Carl planned to spring for a central heating system. Fortunately for him, his brother-in-law, Donald, was experienced in all aspects of homebuilding, including heating, plumbing, and electrical. His main focus was new home construction, but there were no associated installations that were beyond his ability and experience. He readily agreed to install the central heating system for them.

The central heating system was a very big deal for the Raptor family. They had never had such a high-tech heating system and were fairly excited about getting one installed.

The day finally came when Uncle Don pulled up in his work van full of tools and backed up to the door. He had asked for one of the boys to be on hand to help him, and since Randy was working full time at the feed mill, Michael was the best they could provide. Charlotte accurately explained to her brother that Michael could at times have motivational issues, but if a job interested him, he could be a good worker. Uncle Don just gave her a half smile and said he was sure they could make out.

Michael, who was already intrigued by the concept of central heating, was right there and ready to go when the van backed up to the door. Uncle Don opened the rear cargo doors, and there sat the box containing the new furnace. Ever the reader, he read the promotional and statistical information on the box then helped Uncle Don carry it down to the basement. Beside the furnace, there were stacks of gleaming new galvanized sheet metal for the ductwork.

When the furnace was jockeyed into position where it would spend the rest of its life, Uncle Don set up several sawhorses and began to form the ducting by snapping together square and round pipe sections. The metal sheets were crimped along two opposing sides, and he curved the sheets and snapped the crimped edges into each other, creating a round pipe. There were also square duct panels that snapped together for the main ducts out of the furnace heating plenum.

The whole project with its many aspects totally fascinated Michael, and when Uncle Don asked him to hold a duct segment or fetch a certain tool from the many shelves in the van, he hopped to it eagerly. It seemed there were so many special tools that were used to do the coolest things ever to fit all the ducting into each other and pipe the various heat runs up through the floor ducts and through the inside of the walls to the upstairs rooms. Then separate ducts needed to be installed to return the cold air which had been displaced by the warm air, back to the furnace to get heated and circulated back around in the system.

Uncle Don worked without assembly instructions or diagrams. Occasionally, he would pull the carpenter's pencil from behind his ear and perform some calculations on a convenient piece of board, but in his mind, he already knew the size of every duct and where it would be located. He also knew just how everything would be connected to make the system function perfectly.

Michael had never been more impressed by anything in his life! The fact that his uncle could take a furnace in a box and stacks of flat sheet metal and create this masterpiece was to him beyond incredible, and he drank it all in, learning as he went.

Several weeks later when the project was wrapped up, Uncle Don was giving his sister final operating instructions as Michael listened in. "And by the way," Uncle Don said, "I want to hire this young man to replace Carl Jr. since he moved to Pennsylvania."

Charlotte looked shocked and glanced around the room to see if perhaps there was another young man nearby whom her brother was referring to. Finally, her confused gaze came to rest on her third son who had been diligently assisting her brother on the project. "You mean *him*?" she squawked in disbelief.

"Yup," Uncle Don said confidently, "he is a real worker."

Charlotte's face was a mask of bewilderment, wondering how her intelligent brother could have been so hoodwinked when he had worked with her notoriously unmotivated son for nearly three weeks.

"Well, I'm sure we don't have any objection if that's what he wants to do," she finally replied. She couldn't know that this decision would radically change Michael's work ethic for the rest of his life. Working with his uncle who became his mentor and hero gave him an enthusiasm for building things that never left him. In time, he would become known as a hard worker and would even be accused of being a "workaholic."

Michael's new hero looked at him like one man looks at another. "I am starting a new spec house on the other side of Smithville next week," he said conversationally. "I will look for you there Tuesday morning at eight o'clock. Be on time!"

"Okay," Michael replied, feeling ten feet tall, "I'll be there!"

# MENTORED BY A
# BLACK SHEEP

Michael felt a bit trepidatious and very intimidated when his mother dropped him off at the jobsite Tuesday morning. The job site was in a new housing development and several of the nearby lots were in varying stages of new home construction. Uncle Don's new spec house consisted of a freshly poured basement surrounded by large piles of dirt from the excavation. Placed at strategic locations around the basement were truckloads of new lumber stacked on piles nearly as high as Michael was tall. Uncle Don's van was parked on the gravel, which would become the driveway, backed up to the new house basement.

The basement was bisected by a large structural beam resting on tall jacks at the same height of the surrounding walls. Uncle Don instructed Michael to begin carrying lumber from the surrounding stacks and laying them from the basement wall to the support beam where he began nailing them on edge to form the supports for the floor on which the entire house would rest.

It was all very interesting to Michael as the floor of the house began to take shape. When all the support planks had been nailed on edge, they began covering them with four-foot-by-eight-foot sheets of plywood from the huge stack nearby. Uncle Don was working with a smooth, practiced efficiency, pausing only to issue instructions to his new and rather clueless helper. Where he had needed to work off ladders to nail the support planks in place, he now worked on his knees, his hammer rapping out a steady rhythm as he drove the nails through the plywood into the support planking.

Recognizing his nephew's lack of experience, he made a practice of explaining everything he did as he worked. He was relieved to see that Michael was the type of kid who only needed things explained once. He also noted that his new employee could use a bit more muscle tone—something carrying and handling the heavy planks and plywood would soon remedy. Not much physical strength was required to install a new furnace as they had been doing, but framing a new home was something entirely different.

When Charlotte picked him up after work that afternoon, she immediately noticed that he was very tired and sore. She wondered if he would find an excuse to not go to work the next day, but to her surprise, Michael was ready, even eager to get back to work the next morning. The fascination of learning how a new house was built trumped the sore muscles and blisters.

Every step of the new house construction was a new adventure. Uncle Don showed Michael how to nail the two by four wall studs into certain shapes which were called *C*s and *T*s. These would be placed in certain locations in the wall frame to accommodate further framing of the interior walls.

Unlike the furnace project, Uncle Don frequently referred to large blue sheets of paper which he called blueprints. When Michael found time, he perused these blueprints, but they made no sense at all to him. He could see the outline of the house, and some of them showed the layout of future rooms, but most of them were a jumble of lines, numbers, and symbols. It was as confusing as it was interesting.

"Where do you get these from?" Michael asked his uncle one day as they were taking their morning break.

"I made them," Uncle Don replied, then grinned slightly at the look of astonishment on his helper's face.

"Well…what does all this stuff mean?" Michael asked, pointing to the crisscross of lines and symbols.

"Let me show you," his uncle responded, pleased at his new helper's interest. "New home construction has various phases. There is the framing phase which is covered by this top print. Then there are separate prints showing the design for electrical, plumbing, cabinetry, etc. Since it is not possible to fit all the details on one blueprint, a separate print is drawn for each phase. If a contractor decides to hire out something like the plumbing or electrical work, he gives a copy of that blueprint to the subcontractor, so he knows what is required."

"Are you going to hire a subcontractor?" Michael asked, hoping the answer would be no. He wanted to learn all there was to know about building a house.

Uncle Don reached into his shirt pocket and pulled out a pack of cigarettes. "Nope," he replied, pulling a cigarette from the pack and sticking it in his mouth. "We're gonna do this one all by ourselves."

Michael liked the way he had been included in the "ourselves" comment. He sipped his water as his uncle lit his cigarette.

Uncle Don was the official black sheep of the Reynolds family—a label which he wore with not the slightest regret. He had left the Mennonite culture and married a "town girl" and joined the Baptist church. Although the Baptists were arguably the closest denomination in practice to the Mennonites, they still allowed certain things that were an absolute taboo to the Mennonites. They allowed women to trim their hair—a practice that was absolutely forbidden among Mennonites.

Mennonite girls wore their hair in braided pigtails until they became old enough to wear it coiled in a bun on the back of their heads. When they repented of their sins and confessed Jesus as their Lord and savior, they then began to cover the buns with the ubiquitous white mesh "coverings." Some of the women unfortunate enough to have extra-long hair had to endure the indignity later in life of living with a bald spot on their heads where the heavy hair bun had destroyed the hair roots. Fortunately, there were no rules against baldness.

Few, if any, of the Mennonites would come right out and say that a woman who did not wear a covering would end up in Hell, but their teaching and indoctrination was so powerful that that was exactly what most of their children grew up believing. Few, if any, of their parents and elders would attempt to disabuse them of that belief either, and Mennonite girls grew up expecting to wear the white bonnet all their lives.

Uncle Don's wife, Elaine, trimmed her hair and wore no covering. She stood out from the rest of the women at family gatherings, causing the older kids to ask their parents awkward questions about her eternal destiny and apparent life of debauchery. While the family would not openly consign their brother and sister-in-law to the flames of future perdition, they left their children thinking that was where their errant uncle and "worldly" aunt were headed if they didn't see the light and join the Mennonite church.

Michael never understood why Uncle Don smoked. He often found half-smoked cigarettes laying on the lumber framing of the house that had left charred tracks where the rest of the burning cigarette had smoldered until the tobacco burned out. He was amazed that these had never started the house on fire.

In years to come, he would come to hate cigarettes for the filthy, destructive addiction they created in people, but for now, he chose not to overthink it. People could throw all the nasty smear they wanted at his mentor. None of them had ever treated him with the respect and dignity this "black sheep" uncle had, and his loyalty was solid.

It was fortunate for him that there was no communication between him and his parents. If they had caught on to how deeply their son was being impacted by this "black sheep" uncle, they would have without question not allowed Michael to continue working for him. The irony was that while the Mennonite family continued to besmirch and denigrate Uncle Don for his degenerate ways, Michael never once heard him slander them back. There were times when he would make ironic comments letting Michael know that it might be a good idea to compare the prevailing Mennonite dogma with actual scripture, but within his hearing, he remained above the mudslinging.

# SHOP CLASSES

As summer wound down, the days became shorter and cooler. The tree leaves began to turn spectacular fall colors which would be on full display until they dropped off for the cold winter months.

Michael was looking forward to the coming school year. In addition to spending time with Miss Sherri, he would be eligible for driver's education and the full range of industrial arts classes. He signed up for as many as he could fit into his schedule. But the big one was driver's education. He would not turn sixteen until near the end of the school year, so he had to wait for the second class which took place the second half of the school year.

Now that he could play guitar, getting his driver's license was his main goal in life. He packed the year with a woodworking, agriculture, and the first of two welding courses. The woodworking class proved to be the most interesting, followed by the welding class.

The agriculture class was interesting at times but could also be a bit boring. They learned a lot about different soils and their varying chemical and nutritional makeups. One of the more interesting exercises was when they learned to test soil using test tubes and different chemical substances to measure nitrogen, phosphorous, and potassium as well as acidity and pH levels.

The instructor, Mr. Burbank, did a good job of making even the more humdrum aspects of the class relevant, but there was only so much he could do with the unexciting nature of the subject materials. Things like animal husbandry and machinery made the course a bit more practical and interesting. But it was hard for that course to compete with the hands-on, interactive courses like woodworking and welding.

The welding course instructor was a young, mild-mannered man named Mr. Anson, who also served as the assistant instructor for the woodworking courses. Michael took an immediate liking to him and his unassuming nature. Before the first class session, he took his students on a walk-through tour of the facility. Michael was amazed at the huge display of well-cared-for tools and machinery! His father's tools were a collection of broken, rusty castoffs barely adequate to their tasks. Uncle Don had taken care of his tools, but the work they had been doing hadn't required the use of many differing types of tools.

This facility contained shelves loaded with every type of metal working tool and cutter imaginable, as well as a few unimaginable ones. The walls were loaded with hanging hand tools, with their outlines drawn on the pegboard behind them. The floor was covered with strategically spaced welders of every kind. Michael hadn't known that more than one type of welder even existed! All he had ever seen or heard of were the small Lincoln arc welders commonly referred to as "stick welders" or "buzz boxes."

These were rather compact box shaped machines which ran on 220 volts of electricity. Two heavy cords protruded from the front of the welder. One was marked negative and was usually about ten feet long with a large spring-loaded clamp on the end for attaching it to the work. The other cord was about five feet longer and marked positive. It had a handle on the outer end with a small, spring-loaded mouth-like clamp for holding an electrode, commonly referred to as a welding rod. The clamp could be opened or closed by pressing a short attached lever located near the thumb on the handle.

When the ground clamp was attached and the electrode clamped in the holder, the person welding would don a helmet with a very dark lens and touch the electrode to the work, creating a sizzling sound and an extremely bright light.

Michael had tried his hand at welding with the Svenson's machine, then later their own, but he had no idea how the welding process worked or what actually happened within the metal as the welding was in progress. By the end of this course, he would be amazed at what all he had learned.

While the students would have much preferred to have their instructor just turn them loose with the welders and explain how to use them, the approach to their education was much more methodical and organized. They were issued fairly large and well-illustrated textbooks which explained the intricate dynamics of joining two pieces of steel by welding. The students were surprised at how many different types of weld could be made by the same welder, using different electrodes and tactics. They learned what happened to the molecules inside the steel when the welding process took place.

Michael, like most people, had always thought of pieces of steel as hard, solid objects with no moving parts. It was fascinating to learn how the heated sections of steel came alive and animated with the application of intense heat. As the hard steel turned to a molten puddle, the animated molecules within swirled and flowed, looking for their place to resettle and become solid again.

While the molecules themselves were too tiny to see, the person welding could observe the swirl of the puddle of melted steel at the working end of his electrode. How well he guided the flow of the puddle would determine the appearance and strength of his finished weld.

Guiding the electrode was the tricky part of arc welding. The person welding could not simply hold the electrode down on the surface of the steel and expect it to weld for him. The process was called arc welding for a reason. It was necessary to touch the electrode to the metal for a split second to create contact then pull it away approximately one eighth of an inch to create an arc of high voltage electricity which created the intense heat necessary for the process. He then needed to maintain that gap consistently even as he moved the electrode slowly and smoothly along the surfaces to be joined. All the while, the electrode was feeding into the molten puddle, thus rapidly becoming shorter, which also changed the operational dynamics.

The art of striking that arc then pulling it back to maintain an arc without losing the electrical contact was the single most difficult part of the process to master. If the electrode was allowed one second too much time of contact, it would fasten itself to the steel, creating a short circuit in the voltage flow. When this happened, the welder would protest with a loud and continual buzz, announcing to every-one nearby that the rookie using it had once again failed to strike a working arc. It would be necessary for said rookie to give the elec-trode holder a strong twisting jerk to dislodge it so he could try again.

Michael found this process as difficult to master as did his class-mates. Mr. Anson kept telling his young charges not to overthink this process and showed them repeatedly how simple it could be. "Hey guys," he said one day, "how hard do you want to make this? That welder can weld by itself and lay a pretty good bead too!"

His frustrated students looked at him in total disbelief. "Oh, oh," he said with a slight grin. "I don't think you fellows believe me!"

He placed two pieces of steel side by side on the welding table and inserted a new electrode into the nearest welder lead. Then he carefully adjusted the placing of the electrode clamp adjacent to the surface to be welded. "Put your helmets on, guys," he instructed, "so you can watch."

The students complied, and he ever so carefully struck the nec-essary arc and began the weld bead. "Now take off your helmets and look at me," he instructed when the welder was emitting the sizzle of a bead being laid.

The students followed his instructions, and to their utter amaze-ment, he was standing with his hands in his pockets while the welder was pushing itself along the surface of the steel, holding its arc all the while! "It won't go real long by itself," he said as he picked up the holder and stopped the connection. "But as you can see, it does a pretty good job without help!"

Michael couldn't know it then, but he was looking at a major part of his professional future. He would burn tens of thousands of electrodes in his future career and impress many young men and a few young women by the trick Mr. Anson had just showed them as he taught them how to master the arc welder!

The woodworking course was interesting and very informative, although the teacher, a Mr. Bricker, was a gruff and rather intimidat-ing man. His features made him look like he wore a perpetual scowl and his lower lip protruded enough to give him the appearance of a continual pout. Michael found him intimidating even though he had on numerous occasions seen him chatting and joking with other teachers. He was, however, a very well qualified teacher.

They began as usual in the classroom, learning about different species of wood and their properties and which made the best furniture and which were used for framing and decking etc. Then each student was instructed to choose a piece of furniture to build for their class project. Michael decided to build a stereo console out of mahogany. It was a time when stereos were incorporated into large pieces of furniture with big speakers discharging their sound out the front.

The woodworking shop was as impressive as the welding shop, with an impressive array of tools and equipment hanging on the walls and filling shelves and cabinets. The one section was stocked with hundreds of dried lumber boards, including walnut, cherry, pine, mahogany, and other types.

The wood was rough and crooked, and the first step was to saw the edges straight so they could be glued together. Mr. Bricker explained that if you try to use too wide a piece of lumber, it will warp and ruin your furniture, so the boards were sawed into strips of four inches or less then glued edge to edge with long clamps holding them until the glue was dry. Then the clamps were removed and the excess glue was scraped off with a chisel and the real work began. Using a hand planer and sanding blocks, the panel was gradually worked smooth until passing your hand over them felt like sliding it over a windowpane. Some of the panels had small dips and irregularities, and Michael found one in one of his panels. He was examining it when Mr. Anson, the assistant instructor, came by.

"Let me show you how to take care of that dip," he offered. He squeezed a thin layer of wood glue into the hole then told Michael to fill it up with sawdust from his sanding. When Michael had the dip level full, Mr. Anson spread another light layer of sawdust over it then told him to leave it dry then sand it smooth. Unfortunately, Mr. Anson hadn't been gone long when the formidable Mr. Bricker came by and noticed the blemish.

"What did you do, fill that dip with sawdust?" he asked, his tone making it obvious that he was very unimpressed!

"Yeah," Michael admitted. He wanted very much to add that that was what Mr. Anson had told him to do but did not want him to be the object of Mr. Bricker's scorn, so he left him out of it.

"That will never work," Mr. Bricker snapped. But when he ran his finger over the blemish, he turned suddenly more positive. "Did you mix glue in with it?" he asked. Michael nodded dumbly and was relieved when Mr. Bricker grudgingly muttered, "Well, that might work," and moved on to the next table. Michael hadn't realized that Mr. Anson had witnessed the exchange until he stopped by a bit later and asked if Mr. Bricker had accepted that repair method. He seemed appreciative that Michael had kept him out of the exchange, and Michael was very glad he had not tried to pass the buck on to him.

As the weeks passed, the stereo console took shape. There were two small doors in front for storing media inside, and the entire top lifted to access the stereo. Michael was at a loss as to what he could use to cover the large speakers on each side of the cabinet front. Mr. Bricker suggested that he bring in clean burlap from feed sacks. That idea seemed kind of weird, but since he could not come up with a better idea, Michael brought in some burlap and was pleasantly surprised with how well it blended with the rich, dark mahogany of the finished console.

The day finally arrived that Michael and many of his classmates had been so eagerly anticipating—the beginning of the driver's education class. Mr. Burbank who had been their agriculture class teacher was also the driver's education instructor. The first session opened with a film about the responsibilities of operating a motor vehicle, and the opening picture was a single car key. Every student in the class sat silently salivating for the opportunity to stick that key in the ignition of a car and *drive!*

But as always, the course started with a large amount of book and classroom education. It was several months until Michael was able to finally go into the Bureau of Motor Vehicles and take the written test required to obtain a driving permit. He passed the test the first time, and eagerly awaited his turn for the on-road driving lessons.

The high-tech driving simulators were also a huge adventure for this class of future motorists. They provided a very realistic setting where students could make mistakes without damaging property or endangering lives.

But what they were all the most excited about was actually getting behind the wheel of the shiny new car with the big sign above the roof that said *student driver*. The car was provided on loan by a Smithville auto dealership, and it was accessorized by an extra brake pedal on the front passenger side for the instructor to push if a driving lesson went seriously sideways. The boys had an advantage over most of the girls because many of them were farm boys who had been driving tractors since they were quite young. Driving a tractor was enjoyable, but certainly nothing to be compared to the thrill of cruising down the road behind the wheel of an automobile!

When the course was completed and the students had all passed, there remained yet one big hurdle—the official driving test. It needed to be scheduled with the BMV, and Michael was very intimidated by the whole procedure. When the fateful day came for his test, Charlotte drove him to the BMV and helped him check in. The instructor then took charge and ushered him out to the official testing car at the curb. Michael was tense and a bit awkward as he followed the instructor's commands. He was trying to be so cautious that at one time, the instructor told him to speed up or he was going to cause an accident.

When it was over, the instructor gave no indication of whether he had passed or not until they were reunited with Charlotte. Then he gave her the rundown of how the test had gone, and Michael's heart sank a bit lower every time the instructor named another thing that "he needs work on." He got very little opportunity to practice driving at home. Carl was a bit more receptive to his continual badgering to be allowed to drive than was his mother. She made it fairly plain that he could ride a bicycle all his life for all she cared! But she did occasionally let him drive and took him for his test.

When the instructor had finally finished recounting his observations of Michael's imperfect driving skills, he turned to look directly at him and said, "So…I would say…have him work on a few of these things…and I will pass him today!"

Michael couldn't believe his ears! He would forever wonder if the instructor had deliberately popped his balloon just to see his reaction when he passed him! But it didn't matter at all now. He walked out of the BMV with a legal license to operate a motor vehicle on a public highway. Life was good!

# "THERE IS NO OTHER BOSS!"

The next summer, Uncle Don decided to hire more help. "You got any friends that want to work?" he asked Michael in his rumbling bass voice.

"I'll ask around," Michael said, thinking immediately of his church friend Donnie Kurtz. He knew Donnie had been working at the local lumber yard and didn't much like his job.

When he saw Donnie on Sunday, he asked him if he would be interested and Donnie immediately stated that he was. That week, he stopped by the job site for an interview, and two weeks later, he came to work. He and Michael enjoyed working together and often competed against each other driving nails and carrying materials.

Donnie, however, had one thing Michael could absolutely not compete with—a green, 350cc Honda motorcycle. He rode it to work every day and told Michael he should buy a motorcycle so they could ride together.

"We aren't allowed to get a car until we are eighteen," Michael said.

"It's not a car," Donnie said. "It's a motorcycle. I know where there is a real nice Yamaha 180 for sale. It is in like new condition, and the price is really reasonable."

That afternoon when Charlotte came to pick him up, Michael pointed out Donnie's motorcycle and said that if he could get one, she wouldn't have to bother taking him to work every day. To his utter surprise, his parents talked it over, and Carl took him to see the Motorcycle. It was a two-cycle oil injected 180 Yamaha in like new condition as Donnie had said.

After they had looked it over good, Michael paid the asking price and rode it home. He was stunned that his parents had signed off on the idea, even though he realized that his mother was probably tired of hauling him to work and back.

Ownership of his own transportation, however, did little to expand Michael's personal liberties. He had to get permission virtually every tie he fired it up. It was used to take him to work and back and that was all. Once the initial thrill was worn off a bit, Randy began to pester him to trade rides for work. He said his gas guzzling 442 was draining him and he had to drive more than twenty miles a day while Michael only had to drive across town.

The fun of driving the sports car with the thundering power plant under the hood usually convinced Michael to comply.

"Well, Michael," Uncle Don announced one morning, "it looks like we might be getting real busy soon." He went on to explain that the Housing and Urban Development (HUD) department was planning to build a series of new houses in Smithville for low income residents, and he was planning to bid on the project. He would need a lot more labor, so his plan was to form a company together with Uncle Laverne and his son Cousin Henry, who was also on his own in the carpentry business. They would be the three owners with Uncle Don as the chief. The venture was destined for spectacular failure.

Uncle Don hired a taciturn man named Dick as his foreman, and although he assured Michael that their working relationship would remain the same, Michael was now required to answer to a man who seemed to have a rather surly personality and often snapped at him and administered blunt rebukes.

Dick was a fairly tall man who was so skinny that Uncle Harold commented to Randy that "if you viewed him from the side with his tongue sticking out, he would look like a zipper!" He was experienced in carpenter work but not in what would eventually become known as "human resources" management. As the weeks passed, Michael learned how he wanted things done and the relationship went fairly smoothly.

The first major hiccup in the company was in relation to employee wages. HUD had an absolute minimum pay requirement which would raise Michael's hourly rate by exactly one dollar per hour. Some of Laverne and Henry's men would be in for large increases as well, and it was not sitting well with Uncle Laverne. When he had first been informed of this requirement, he had loudly proclaimed that he would go around to the men on payday and take back the extra increase, to which Uncle Donald had informed him that he would be doing no such thing!

This exchange between them illustrated perfectly the difference in how they viewed their help. It mostly came down to respect but also involved honesty. Some of Laverne's dealings were a bit on the shady side. Michael had once heard him tell a story about how they had been doing a remodel job upstairs in a house and were using the bed for a sawhorse to cut paneling. He had gotten a bit careless and made a rather deep saw cut into the bed. He seemed rather pleased with his own ingenuity as he explained how they flipped the mattress upside down and turned the blanket and bedspread cuts toward the back. "Everything looked in pretty good shape when we left," he said with a chuckle. Michael had been rather shocked. He couldn't imagine Uncle Donald ever doing something like that. The irony struck him again how Uncle Laverne's reputation would be protected by his good church affiliation, but if "bad boy" Uncle Donald had done that, his reputation would have been smeared for months!

The new company had barely begun building when they encountered a paperwork snafu that halted production. Since Uncle Don was tied up full time in working it through, Cousin Henry said he could use Michael for a few days to finish up a roofing job he had going.

The roof turned out to be a very tall barn with a haymow, making the peak nearly forty feet high. Henry had some long ladders but none nearly that long. That small problem was overcome by stretching several of his longest ladders out full length and tying them together with baling twine. It was an all-hands-on-deck challenge lifting, dragging, and sliding the floppy creation up to the roof, but it was finally accomplished. Henry scurried to the top of it and drove several roofing nails partway into the roof then wrapped baler twine around them from the ladder. "Okay," he instructed Michael when he was back on solid ground, "start carrying up shingles, and we will nail them on."

Michael was still gawking at the rickety assembly in stark unbelief! Henry seemed not to notice as he strapped on his tool belt and filled the pouch with nails. Then as if to lead by example, he slung a pack of shingles over his shoulder and scampered up the ladder, as agile as a squirrel. Michael grabbed another pack of shingles, threw it over his shoulder, and began to climb. Climbing was something he had never had much occasion to do in his life, and his trepidation mounted as the wobble of the ladder under him increased. Halfway up, the ladder swayed so badly he wasn't sure he would be able to maintain his grip on it and the shingles. He was sure of one thing though, if he had to let go of something, the pack of shingles was gonna go back down a lot faster than they had come up! He managed to steady the ladder and continued his upward climb to where Henry had nailed a two-by-four to the roof to walk on and was busily nailing on shingles.

When he was back on the ground, Henry's other helper climbed up with his tools and another pack of shingles and began to work alongside Henry. Neither of them showed the slightest trepidation over the fact that they were one slip away from a forty-foot fall.

As the day progressed, Michael got used to the climb and learned how to do it with the least amount of sway in the ladder. Carrying bundle after bundle up the ladder began to take a toll on his legs, however. By the time they paused for noon lunch break, they were aching and sore. He was all too ready to collapse beside the others in the shade of a huge maple tree for thirty minutes of relief.

By afternoon, his legs were aching, and his body was drained of energy. The hot sun was blazing down on them and he was guzzling water on nearly every trip to the ground. *Why can't Henry and Laverne get good jobs like Uncle Don?* he wondered sourly. *Every time I get involved working for them, they have some crap job going, and I am at the bottom of the crap crew! No wonder Dad and Carl Jr. didn't like working for these guys!* He thought of the nice projects he had helped Uncle Don build and appreciated his good fortune that his uncle had chosen him!

Uncle Don soon had the paperwork smoothed out and the HUD project resumed. It was a good job, and the Michael's pay had increased by one dollar per hour due to the HUD minimum pay requirement. But much of the special working relationship and mentoring he had enjoyed with his uncle was now gone. It was just a good job. But there was entertainment for no extra charge. Every so often, Laverne or Henry would show up on their job and issue instructions to Dick and Michael when Uncle Don was not around. They found this confusing because when you receive orders from a company owner, common sense dictated that you comply. Michael told his uncle that it was confusing when you were getting conflicting orders from different bosses, to which Uncle Don roared emphatically, *"I am THE boss, there is no other boss!"*

When Uncle Don got back and discovered them doing things different than he had instructed, his temper would flare, and he would march down to their jobsite and again try to impress on them that he was the ultimate authority and they were not to come around countermanding his orders! These scenes always involved shouting, accusations, and a general pointing out of each other's overall deficiencies. Cousin Henry even used words that were not lawful to be uttered among Mennonite people!

The biggest problem of all was that they took their frustrations home to their wives who freely took sides and gossiped with their siblings about all the problems and irritations that were developing in this ill-advised partnership. One night after work, Michael's mother would have heard one side of the story and be promoting that as the one to believe, then a day or two later, she would have heard the other side and be promoting that perspective. Michael was totally sick and disgusted of having to witness it at work then come home and hear it all re-hashed again. He never willingly offered his mother any information about the mess and finally decided to quit and go to work for a logger.

It was difficult for him to tell his uncle and hero he was going to quit, but he tried to explain to him how difficult it was to live with all the strife. Being well aware of the problematic situation, Uncle Don was disappointed, but he understood and took it well, and Michael was temporarily unemployed.

As the Raptor boys became increasingly involved in social activities with their friends, their home became a common place for socializing. To their credit, Carl and Charlotte were gracious hosts to Glendale youth and older folks alike. The many horses were always a draw for the horse lovers, and many lovely Sunday afternoons would find Randy and Michael saddling up every available horse to take fairly large groups of their friends on horseback tours around the neighborhood, through the forests, and around the farm.

There were also Sunday afternoons when only the Miller girls would come to ride with Randy and Michael. Michael was so addicted to riding horses that he didn't mind his brother using him as a patsy to further his "unofficial" romance. The Miller girls were always fun to be around, and Michael would often end up riding with Bertha while Randy and Rene disappeared into the forest with their horses.

One afternoon, Rene and Bertha were lagging behind, deep in sisterly conversation, and Michael and Randy drifted out of sight ahead of them on the trail. They were trying to think of a prank to pull on the girls. They couldn't pretend to be lost because they were riding on a well-marked logging trail. They finally decided to hide their horses and pretend they had thrown them and ran away. They tied their mounts in a dense thicket and were back on the trail with perplexed looks on their faces when the sisters rounded the bend, deep in conversation.

"What happened?" asked Bertha, somewhat alarmed at the sight of the boys on foot.

"Our horses took off without us," Michael said. "Did you see them?"

"No," Rene replied, "where do you think they went?"

"We'll help you look for them," Bertha said, sliding down from her saddle.

They tied the girls' horses to a tree near the trail and headed into the surrounding woods. The girls began calling the names of their horses as they walked, their concern growing by the minute. "Do you think they will come back?" Rene asked hopefully.

"Well, if nothing else they will end up back at the barn," Randy stated confidently.

*Don't you wish, big brother?* Michael thought dryly. *That way you and little Miss lovebird could ride back double on her horse!*

After leading the girls on a long and circular goose chase in the woods, they ended up back on the logging road where they had begun. Then they led the girls into the nearby thicket to where their horses were patiently waiting, tied to the bushes. The girls, realizing they had been had, began threatening all kinds of retribution. But it was all done in fun, and they would find ample opportunities to repay the Raptor brothers in kind.

Sometimes there would be just one or two who came along for the afternoon. Leighton was a very regular visitor. He had been very close with Randy, and they were still great friends, but their interaction was being strangled a bit by Randy's involvement with Rene. This brought him closer to Michael, and he ended up being a great buddy to both of them.

One of the things the Raptor boys could not get enough of was their mother's delicious pies. Several times she had threatened to make them eat pie for an entire meal.

She made good on this threat one Sunday evening when Leighton happened to be visiting. They were all called to the supper table where they immediately noticed that the normal huge bowls of steaming food were conspicuously absent. There were water cups and silverware at each place setting, but instead of dinner plates, a whole pie sat at each position.

Leighton seemed a bit shocked but was as delighted as the rest of the boys to dig in to this unconventional supper. Charlotte was not surprised to discover that an all-pie supper did nothing to dull their appetite for her pie, and it was all done in good humor.

# DEER HUNTING

Fall had always been Michael's favorite season. The extended Reynolds family had tradition of driving into the hills where the glorious fall foliage was breathtaking. They would all share a picnic lunch then hike higher into the hills. At the pinnacle of the highest hill was an observation tower where the county would post a lookout during times of high risk for forest fires. By the time Michael reached the base of the tower, he was winded and stopped to catch his breath. Several of the older and fitter guys made a point of charging right up the long, winding stairs to the top of the one-hundred-foot-tall tower. When Michael finally huffed and puffed his way to the top, he gazed in awe out over the thousands of acres of forested hills ablaze in all shades of yellow, orange, and red from the leaves ending their oxygen-making phase and falling to begin their composting phase where they would be absorbed into the soil to feed the tree in the continuous cycle of life.

By the time everyone had made their way back to the picnic site, the shadows would be lengthening, and the fall air would have a chilly bite. The days were getting shorter rapidly as the winter approached.

Fall was also deer hunting season. Deer hunting was taken very seriously by most rural folks in the area. Uncle Gary had a lot of good hunting on his farm, and he was very gracious about inviting friends and relatives to form large hunting parties. Michael had scraped together enough cash to buy an old seven millimeter army rifle, and Randy owned a .303 British army rifle of about the same age. They had become reasonably good marksmen with coaching from Uncle Gary but had yet to score their first buck.

The most successful method of hunting deer was to post a row of shooters at the far side of a woods then the rest of the hunters would spread out on a line and drive the deer toward the hunters waiting at the far side. The deer would hang in the cover of the woods as long as they could, but eventually the pressure of the approaching line of hunters at their rear forced them to make a wild dash across the open field where shooters had been posted.

Usually when a deer went down, he would be brought down by one of the posted shooters. But occasionally, one of the drivers would get a shot at a buck who was reluctant to break cover. Some of the hunters claimed that the bucks were smart enough to push the doe out ahead of them in case danger lurked in the open field.

One day, Michael was driving in the row beside Brian Bannon. Before the drive, he had heard Cousin Henry giving Brian a hard time because he only had one bullet left for his ancient Russian made army rifle. "I only plan to shoot one buck," Brian had responded dryly. "What's the point of carrying a bunch of extra ammunition around? Besides, ammo is hard to find for this rifle, and this is the only bullet I have left."

They drove the woods, and near the far edge, Michael saw a fairly large buck leap to his feet and take off in front of him and Brian. They were nearly at the edge of the woods, and the buck had nowhere to go but across the open field. He broke out into the field directly in front of Brian, running flat out for the far side in long, leaping bounds. The uncut grass was as high as his shoulders, and he nearly disappeared in it at the bottom of his bounds. Michael couldn't get a shot, but when he looked over at Brian, he saw him taking careful aim at the disappearing buck. His rifle barrel was moving slightly up and down as he tracked the deer's bounds. When Michael was sure the buck was safely out of range, the large caliber Russian rifle suddenly emitted a loud, sharp boom.

"I think I got him!" Brian shouted. Michael was sure he couldn't have hit the bounding buck from that great a distance, but he joined the other hunters as they fanned out to search the tall grass for him.

Sure enough, about five minutes later, one of the hunters yelled, "I found him!" and they all converged to the spot where the mortally wounded deer was breathing his last. Brian borrowed a rifle to finish him off then began the messy job of field dressing the animal. It was a rather gruesome task, but it went fast with all the experienced help, and soon Brian was headed back for his truck, dragging a winter's supply of venison behind him.

Larger families with multiple hunters would often get several deer each season, and when there was more venison than they could use, it was always shared with others in their church circles, especially widows, elderly couples, or families who had no hunters. Meat taken during hunting and fishing was never wasted.

The next day, Michael was again helping drive a woods when a deer jumped up in front of him. His view was somewhat obstructed by the brush, but he was pretty sure he saw horns on its head, so he snapped off a shot. The deer went down and stayed down, and the hunters gathered around. When Michael looked closer, his heart sank as he saw that the buck's antlers were not long enough to make the three-inch minimum allowed for a buck tag. It could have been legal on a doe tag, but those were hard to get, and there was none available in this hunting party.

"I can't take that home," Michael said. "My folks will have a fit!"

"I'll take it," Henry offered. "Just give me your buck tag, and you can tell them you gave it to me."

Relief surged through Michael, and he gladly handed over his tag. It would be the only deer he would ever shoot, and he couldn't even be proud of his accomplishment. Although it was a fairly common error, the sting of that mistake stayed with him for years. Years later, he compounded his unimpressive hunting saga by trading the seven millimeter rifle to Johnny for a Chevy car motor to replace the oil burner in his rusty ride. When he went to install it, the engine was seized up tight, but he believed Johnny when he told him that it had been running when he parked the car out back of the barn, so he swallowed his disappointment. He had stopped hunting years ago anyway, so he really didn't need the gun.

In spite of the occasional tragedies caused by gun accidents, guns were very common in rural homes and farms. Deer and small game hunting was popular for meat as well as sport, and most children began using guns by their early teens. Michael was as interested in guns as any of his friends, but several gun related incidents had rather freaked him out. The first incident occurred at the Svenson's place. Thad had invited Michael over with a couple other classmates to hang out and maybe do some target shooting. Thad furnished a .22 caliber rifle, and they were shooting at cans and bottles and the occasional bird that flew into their line of sight. Their marksmanship left a lot to be desired, and the birds had little to fear from them. After a while, Thad suggested a new game he had heard of. He demonstrated by wedging live rounds of .22 cartridges into cracks on a wooden fence post, then they stepped back to see if they could hit the cartridges and detonate them. It proved to be very difficult, and they wasted many rounds trying to hit them, until Thad finally managed to detonate one. A while later, a rather chubby boy named Pat scored a hit, but to everyone's shock, the empty cartridge exploded back toward his face, cutting a small but deep round spot on his cheek near his nose. They managed to get the bleeding stopped, but the wound had to be explained to his parents with no mention of guns involved. Michael heard later that he told them he was crawling over a pile of junk and tripped and fell. His parents then deduced that he must have fallen on a small pipe. The boys were all aware that if it had struck him two inches higher, it would have destroyed his right eye. It was rather a shocking lesson to Michael about the power of guns.

The next unsettling experience occurred some months later when he had purchased a used twelve-gauge shotgun. He was strolling around the farm with the loaded shotgun in search of a target when a tiny Chickadee hopped into view. He raised the gun and took careful aim and pulled the trigger. The gun exploded with a deafening boom, and the bird instantly disappeared. It didn't fly away, it simply ceased to exist! Michael carefully searched the ground where it had been but not a feather or a speck of blood could be seen. The powerful load of game shot had totally obliterated it! He found the whole experience rather unsettling.

The worst gun experience of all involved a stray dog that Charlotte wanted rid of. Since the death of the faithful Laddie, they had gone through several dogs, but none could ever measure up to what Laddie had meant to them.

The dog was a fairly large German Shepherd mix who seemed to be absolutely devoid of any redeeming qualities or talents whatsoever. The humane option of euthanizing an animal with barbiturates whereby they slip into a deep and permanent sleep was virtually unheard of in those days. Usually one well-placed shot to the head would be the merciful method of putting them down.

One fateful afternoon, Michael and Randy took the dog out into the woods with the twelve gauge shotgun and several cartridges containing slugs. Randy held the dog leash while Michael placed the muzzle close to the dog's head and pulled the trigger. The gun boomed, and the dog shuddered. A huge hole appeared in the dog's head, but he remained standing, looking directly up at Michael. Shocked, Michael put the gun to his head again and pulled the trigger for a second shot. The second slug blew away a large portion of his head, but the dog remained standing and began to howl a loud, weird sound that chilled Michael's blood. He glanced helplessly at Randy and saw shock on his face that matched his own! He had one cartridge left. He decided to try for a heart shot. He took careful aim and fired again. The dog staggered but remained on his feet, still emitting the dreadful, haunting howl of the doomed.

"Randy," Michael exclaimed in a ragged voice. "You gotta go get some more shells! Get plenty, I don't know what this is gonna take!"

Randy, always the faster runner, sprinted back toward the house while Michael stood there clutching the shotgun and holding the rope of the howling dog. Soon Randy reappeared with a fistful of cartridges which Michael jammed into the gun. The dog was still on his feet but swaying now as the volume of his howl diminished. Several shots later, it was over, and two very relieved boys headed back to the house. What they had just witnessed was basically impossible and deeply disturbing!

# THE QUONSET BARN
# AND LOGGERS

"We have a new project," Carl announced one evening at the supper table. "The neighbor wants rid of his round roof barn, and we can have it for the taking."

There was a bit of discussion while Charlotte and the boys tried to envision which neighbor's barn was to become their newest treasure. "You can't move that barn!" Charlotte exclaimed when she finally figured out which barn it was. "That's a two-story barn!"

"Yup!" Carl said rather smugly. "I got it all figured out. We will cut the top story off and haul it separately, then we will have two single-story barns."

"And just how are you going to get the top story down to ground level?" Charlotte inquired. "Do you have a helicopter lined up maybe?" The sarcasm in her words and tone was unmistakable. But Carl seemed oblivious to her skepticism.

We will take some bumper jacks and jack up the roof with some posts then drag the bottom story out from under it then let the roof down and haul it on the pickup.

Now the whole family was staring at him like he had lost his mind! They had gotten somewhat used to his wild ideas over the years, mainly because he would nearly always figure out a way to make them work in spite of a myriad of unintended consequences along the way to his goals.

Work began immediately on the barn moving project. Carl rounded up a half-dozen-old style bumper jacks and fastened extensions on them to reach the roof. When they were all secured, they began to jack them all together. The native lumber creaked and groaned as they jacked and pried the roof loose from the haymow floor. When it was finally completely loose, they drug the bottom story out from under it, leaving it wobbling in midair. Carefully, they began to jack it down until it was only about two feet from the ground. Then Carl cut an opening in one end large enough to back his trusty Dodge pickup under it with only the hood and windshield sticking out. Then they nailed timbers across the pickup bed from one side of the roof to the other to support it for transport. The seriously overloaded half ton pickup was squatting badly, but with a bit more air in the tires, the several mile journey to the Raptor farm began.

To describe the spectacle of a twenty-foot-wide round barn roof going down the road with the hood and windshield of a Dodge pickup peeking out in front of it as weird would be a gross understatement. By some minor miracle they made it to the Raptor farm without incident. Several weeks later, the structure was serving as a horse barn. It was in this structure that Michael would receive his last beating at the age of sixteen.

While Michael was not singularly impressed with his father's ingenuity in that project, it did help cement one of the two life lessons in his mind that he would learn from him. One was that there is *always* a way to do what needs to be done, and the other was that you can usually make what you need with the materials you have available with some creative adaptation. He did, however take exception to Carl's total lack of concern for esthetics. He liked completed projects to be neat, solid, and attractive, not the ugly cobbled together creations which seemed to satisfy his father. But those two lessons would serve him well in his adult life as a building contractor.

Randy had a new job. He had been hired by Charlotte's brother, Uncle Harold, who was a logger. Uncle Harold had been in the logging business most of his adult life. He had a large family with five sons of his own whom he had taught to work with him in the logging business. He was known as a smart, hardworking man who had built some of his own logging machinery and was very knowledgeable in hydraulics. One story that had circulated about him was that he had a love for 7 Up soda, but with such a large family, he could not afford to keep it on hand. He hit upon the idea of keeping a stash of it in the cold stream running through his farm. One day, his sons were playing in the stream and discovered his 7 Up stash. They wanted to drink it so badly but knew that if he found it missing, he would be very upset. So they hit upon the idea of drinking the soda then refilling the bottles with the clear stream water. They had a great time drinking the soda pop then refilled the bottles and carefully reinstalled the lids and placed them back into the stream.

When their father discovered what they had done, he was so impressed with their ingenuity that he didn't even punish them for their transgression. He got a lot of enjoyment out of telling that story over the years.

Randy enjoyed working for Uncle Harold and his strength from working in the feed mill was very helpful in the rugged logging industry. He purchased a chain saw and learned how to cut down or "fell" trees, then cut the limbs off and cut the tops off. Then one of Uncle Harold's sons would hook a half dozen of the trimmed trees behind a large four-wheel drive log skidder and drag them out to a clearing where someone would be waiting with a chainsaw to cut them into lengths and stack them with a hydraulic loader. The stacks of logs would often loom higher than the big diesel trucks, which rumbled in on the logging trails to haul them to market. Hauling the logs was Uncle Harold's job until some of his older children got old enough to learn how to safely load and haul the heavy loads.

Negotiating the logging roads could be very tricky and even dangerous at certain times of the year. If the weather was rainy, the trails would be soft and muddy, and the heavy trucks would sink to their axels and get stuck, blocking the one lane trail. In the winter, they would be solid but often slick with packed snow and ice. Much of the area was hilly, and the heavy trucks would often lose traction and steering control on the hills and slide off into the ditches. Nearly every aspect of the industry was dangerous, and most of the men engaged in it were injured and more than a few even lost their lives. The most common injuries were from saws kicking back and cutting gashes in the loggers' legs. The biggest danger, however, came from trees or parts of trees getting hung up in neighboring trees, which would then have to also be cut down with the logger working directly under the hung up tree. When the second tree began to fall, the hung-up tree would dislodge, and the logger would have mere seconds to dash for safety before it crashed directly where he had stood to drop the second tree. In the winter, the snow would be anywhere from knee deep to hip-deep, making the dash to safety carrying the still running chain saw very difficult. If the logger tripped, the first tree would crash down on top of him.

One afternoon, Randy came home from work early with a slight limp. He had had an accident when his saw had kicked back and gouged a furrow in his leg. He had been to the doctor and gotten it stitched, but he had to take it easy for the next few days to allow the wound to heal. Another time he had a very close call when a large tree branch which had broken off and gotten lodged in the limbs of neighboring trees came loose and smashed down on him, shattering his hardhat. There was no doubt that his hardhat saved his life that day.

Overall though, Randy enjoyed the work, and the pay was excellent. He always got along well with Uncle Harold whose boys were heard to complain that he treated Randy better than he did his own boys, to which he retorted that Randy usually showed him more respect than his own boys did!

One evening, Randy came home and announced at the supper table that he had earned fifty dollars that day. That was an enormous amount of money in a day when the average wage in their state was three dollars and fifty-eight cents per hour.

# THE COMBINE

The Raptor farm was not a typical area farm. Most of the farmers were serious about wrestling a livelihood out of their farms. There were vastly differing approaches to how they went about it, but the one thing they all shared in common was their total dedication to their farming occupations. While some of them tried to get by spending as little money as possible on equipment and upgrades, others at the other end of the scale would borrow money they could not afford to pay back to buy and maintain shiny new equipment. Some of the more ambitious young men would take on part time jobs to help them get started.

Carl and Charlotte were not serious about trying to make a living off their small farm. They had tried that route back in South Dakota, and it had not worked out for them. But they wanted to live in the country and raise their family on a farm, so this eighty-acre farm fit their needs well. About a third of the land was wooded, and much of the open ground was in pasture, but there was some acreage available for planting which they did each year. One year, they planted corn with a bunch of antiquated tillage and planting equipment. The corn crop turned out fair, but they had no combine for harvesting. Carl's low-tech solution was to hitch the horses to a wagon and collect the family to pluck and husk the ears by hand and throw them onto the wagon. It was interesting and rather fun for the first couple days, but it got tedious real fast. They had little impromptu contests to try to break the mind-numbing tedium, but those got old as well. Someone came up with the old joke that they should keep two ears in the air at all times. The punchline was, of course, the ears on his head, not the ears sailing into the wagon.

The following year, Randy and Michael convinced their father to plant oats. They worked the ground and located an old planter they could borrow, and soon the oats were growing nicely. True to form, no one gave any real serious consideration to how they would harvest the oat crop. Back in South Dakota, they had had a sheaf binder which would cut the oats or wheat and bundle it into arm-ful-sized bundles, which it would wrap in string and discharge on the ground behind it. When the field was harvested, it would be littered with these small bundles, and it would be necessary for the farmers to go through the field manually and collect these bundles and stand them on end in a circular arrangement with several bundles across the top to shed water. When finished, the field looked like an Indian village with miniature golden teepees. Then the man who owned the threshing machine would make the rounds in the community, setting up behind one barn after another to separate the grain from the straw in the bundles. He had a huge, ancient two-cylindered tractor which emitted a continuous series of loud, rapid pops when it ran. He would stretch a flat drive belt from a round pulley on his tractor to the round pulley on the threshing machine, and the huge machine would roar into life. The neighbors would gather together with their teams and wagons to haul the bundles to the machine which would hungrily gobble them up then dispense a steam of bright yellow grain from an auger on one side, and blow out the golden straw on the other side. It was fun for the community but a tremendously inefficient way to harvest grain.

Here in Ohio, as in most other farm states, the farmers had combine machines to pull behind their tractors which would cut and thresh the grain all at once, spitting the straw out the rear and collecting the grain into a hopper, which would be transferred into a wagon to take to the storage bins on the farm. Some of the more progressive farmers even had self-propelled combines which required no tractor but were operated from a seat mounted on the machine itself.

In the absence of a sheaf binder, Randy and Michael offered to go together and buy an old pull-behind combine, and Carl agreed to give them part of the profit from the grain to make it worth their while. They searched and finally located an ancient machine and brought it back to the farm. All of them including Carl were completely new to the operation of a combine. Carl was good at fixing the old sheaf binders, but they had little in common with the more technologically advanced combines. Carl, Randy, and Michael were all a bit excited to try the machine out, so they hitched it behind a tractor and headed out to the field.

It didn't work! The machine cut the grain off okay, but when the straw spat out the back, much of the grain came out with it. They had no idea how to adjust the machine, and their father, usually their fount of knowledge, was equally clueless. Darkness was approaching fast and they were getting frustrated. Randy began making some adjustments which seemed to help some, but the final product was still unacceptable.

The next evening, they were invited to a picnic where several of Charlotte's farming brothers-in-law were in attendance. Michael and Randy decided to tell them about their problem and ask their advice on how to adjust the machine. They were barely finished telling their tale of woe, when one of the uncles looked at Carl and suggested that he'd better go help them get it working. He looked a bit flustered and said, "Yeah, I didn't check it and they took it out and tried to use it."

Michael was flabbergasted. Never in his life had he ever to his knowledge, heard either of his parents flat-out lie! He wouldn't have believed it possible! In spite of several lies their family had been living, outright lying was one of the most egregious crimes in their family, and he had been whipped numerous times for lying, including a time or two when he had been innocent! He glanced at Randy and saw a look of shock on his face too. Even Johnny seemed to be perplexed. They kept their silence, however. It took little imagination to visualize the painful consequences any of them would have experienced had they exposed the lie!

Later, as Michael was pondering this incident, he recalled another confusing incident with his mother. She had told him many times that the worst thing a child can do is talk bad about his mother. He had believed that nearly all his life, and one morning when she dropped the children off for summer Bible school, she warned them not to say anything bad about her.

"That's the worst thing we can do, isn't it?" Michael remarked.

His mother regarded him closely with a stern look on her face. "Why do you say that?" she asked suspiciously.

"Well, that's what you tell us," he responded defensively.

He was relieved when she finally let it drop, but he was very confused about why she had made an incident about it. It would be much later when the dots connected in his mind and realize that she had made that up and thought he was mocking her that morning. Her reaction to him quoting it made him realize that she had known all along that it was "propaganda." He had often heard the saying that "everybody lies" but had never really believed it. Living with his parents' strict moral code, he had just assumed that they did not have it in them to be dishonest. He had surely been whipped hard enough and often enough for his dishonesty. In years to come, he would understand that everyone has human weaknesses, and everyone fails occasionally in one way or another! *(Thank you very much, Adam and Eve!)*

# ZACHARY KRUGER

Junior year school that fall was very different. Michael was a high school junior, and the upper classes were afforded a lot of privileges and liberties in the new school. One of these included romancing inappropriately all over the campus. They were now in what was called a "free study" system where there were no study halls, and all one needed to do was show up for their forty-five-minute classes.

One guy named Zachary Kruger was a grade ahead of Michael. Like many of the students he lived on a farm, but his father was more of a "shade tree mechanic" than he was a farmer. Their farm looked like a salvage yard with all makes and models of junked vehicles scattered around in a haphazard fashion. Since many people in the area worked on their own vehicles, they would often come to the Kruger farm for used parts off the retired vehicles. Michael got to be casual friends with Zachary, and one evening after school, he was at their place when someone came who wanted a starter Bendix for a Chevy car. They checked the Chevy cars, and none of them had the necessary Bendix.

As they were walking out in defeat, Michael noticed all the auto parts half buried in the dirt where they had been dropped or cast aside over the years. "Hey, there's one!" Zachary yelped and bent down and pulled a half-buried Bendix out of the mud.

Michael looked at him like he had lost his mind. "How do you know that is the right part?" he asked dubiously. "It's not even on a vehicle."

"Well, it is obviously a Chevy Bendix," Zachary insisted, "and they are all the same for that year and several years before and after, so I'm sure it will work!"

Michael was pretty sure his buddy just wanted the few bucks from the sale, but he buttoned his lip and watched as Zachary wiped some of the dirt from the part and exchanged it for a few dollars. He was amazed a few days later when Zachary reported to him that the guy had installed it and it had worked well.

Zachary was from a family whose lifestyle would one day be labelled as "redneck." They drove old noisy cars which they were constantly working on and had several extra vehicles in varying states of disrepair scattered around their house, most of which had at least one jack or block holding them up. The tires on the vehicles he drove sported as much tread as the average sausage casing. Once, before climbing in for a ride with Zachary, Michael pointed out one of the tires which seemed exceptionally bereft of tread. Zachary walked around the car to examine the tire then looked at Michael like he had clearly lost his mind.

"What are you talking about?" he demanded indignantly. "There is a lot of life left in that tire, there isn't one bit of the cord showing yet!"

Michael shook his head in disbelief and crawled on in. *He was used to his father cobbling things, but at least he kept tread on the car tires!*

One story being told around school was how Zachary tried to buy a 1957 Chevy Impala. The 1957 Impala hardtop was becoming a classic, and he had the opportunity to buy one for five hundred dollars. Although that was a good deal, Zachary didn't have anywhere near that much money, so he went to see his banker with whom his track record of loan repayment was less than admirable. As the story went, Zachary walked into his office and announced that he wanted to borrow five hundred dollars to buy a 1957 Chevy. The banker stared at him for a moment then stabbed his finger in the direction of the door and said, "Kruger, *out!*" The gregarious Zachary slunk out in defeat, and the bargain purchase opportunity passed him by.

On the other end of the spectrum was a handsome young man named Ricky Danner who came from a fairly affluent family. Ricky drove a gorgeous 1955 two-door hardtop customized Chevy with a flawless, gleaming coat of orange paint. The car sported hood scoops, black striping, and most impressive of all, the exhaust pipes had been customized to vent out black built-in ports low in the sides of the car just ahead of the rear wheel wells. It was a work of art on wheels, and Ricky drove it like a wild man, especially when he had been drinking.

Ricky was a senior, and a reasonably nice guy who pretty much had his pick of the girls. Michael did not see a lot of him around school because they weren't in the same classes and had virtually nothing in common except an affection for snazzy cars and cute girls. The gossip around the school was that Ricky couldn't stand his older brother's fiancé. The upcoming wedding was scheduled a couple months before graduation, and Ricky could not reconcile himself to having her for a sister-in-law. He had been close with his brother and had told him, "I'll die if you marry that girl!" But his brother had a very different opinion of her, and wedding plans proceeded full speed ahead.

The night of the wedding, Ricky got very drunk, then jumped in his car for a wild ride home. He never made it home. The gorgeous orange car left the road and smashed into a bridge at a high rate of speed, and Ricky died behind the wheel that night.

The shock of the tragedy went through the entire school. Many students remembered his emphatic declaration that "he would die if his brother married that girl!" He had died that same night!

One of the teachers who would impact Michael's life the most this year was the awe-inspiring Mr. Marconi. Ron Marconi was a young, handsome Italian who might well have been the inspiration for the future TV show *Fonzi*. Virtually all the students, male and female, idolized him, and Michael suspected that half of the female teachers were attracted to him for reasons having nothing to do with his mechanical genius. He taught courses in auto mechanics, power mechanics, and small engine repair. Michael, of course, signed up for all three.

Mr. Marconi was a professional auto racer who raced on straight tracks at extremely high rates of speed. There was a rumor that he had once lost a steering tie rod at 175 miles per hour while racing.

His race car was a Dodge with a souped-up 426 Hemi engine. It was a deep, metallic purple with the name "Plum Crazy" emblazoned on both sides in bright yellow letters. He had shaved the heads and added a turbocharger, which at that time was used only for racing cars. His racing tires were "slicks," which meant they were as bereft of tread as Zachary's but had about one inch of solid rubber instead of tread. He wanted the widest tires available but could not find rims wide enough for them that would fit his car. He solved the problem by widening the car rims himself using the school's modern welding and tool-and-die equipment. Since his racing slicks were designed for only seven pounds-per-square-inch or PSI of air pressure instead of the normal thirty-five to forty pounds PSI, he used sheet metal screws to fasten the tires to the rims so they wouldn't spin inside the tires with the huge amount of horsepower driving them.

Occasionally, Mr. Marconi would park his race car outside the industrial arts building if he was doing some after-hours work on it. Several times, Michael heard him start it up, and it was incredibly loud.

While the guys at school were content to remain awestruck over the powerful machine, Zachary took it to another level. He bought some aerosol cans of purple paint and gave his rolling wreck of a car a new paint job. Then he took a can of yellow and painted "plum crazy" on both sides in huge letters. Michael thought the whole effect was garish and pathetic! But he prudently kept his opinion to himself in a rare display of self-control.

In the power mechanics course, the students were taught the basics of mechanization, from the invention of the wheel and how it transformed the human existence over time, to the harnessing of fire and how amazingly that led to such marvelous inventions as furnaces and the wonder of the internal combustion engine. There were, of course, more sinister adaptations such as the weapons of warfare, but they were not the focus of the power mechanics course. Michael was spellbound as Mr. Marconi described how people learned how to turn straight motion into rotary motion by a piston arm attached to a wheel and how gears allowed much more flexibility in adapting power sources to the work needing performed. In years past, people would attach a fifteen-foot lone pole horizontally to a machine requiring power such as for grinding grain, etc. They would then hitch a horse or mule to the outer end of the pole and make them walk in circles for hours, pulling the pole attached to the machine and creating a circular power input.

Mr. Marconi also touched on the evolution of controlling the fuel input to the power source to achieve the needed amount of power output. He described how gasoline engines were controlled by the operator through use of a carburetor, an ingenious device containing tiny ports and passageways to feed the hungry internal combustion engine. This, of course, led to an explanation of how the fuel was ignited to cause the millions of mini explosions inside the cylinders which created the power output. An intricate electrical system delivered short, powerful bursts of electricity to the spark plugs protruding into the gas-filled cylinder heads which ignited the fuel and sent the cylinder down on its "power stroke." It was all awe-inspiring even if it was a bit mind-boggling. Mr. Marconi assured them that much more detail would be forthcoming for those who signed up of the auto mechanics and small engines courses.

The metal-working course, taught by Mr. Burbank, included another totally foreign industry known as Tool-and-Die. The huge machinery used for this course allowed one to shave and machine chunks of steel into all kinds of interesting shapes and forms. There were the milling machines for shaving steel to precise measurements known as millimeters. A millimeter was described as the distance a railroad rail would sag if a fly landed on it. Michael was rather suspicious that that description was an exaggeration, but he never was quite certain.

Other machines known as lathes were used to turn chunks of steel in a rotary motion while shaving it down to exact round diameters. This machine also had attachments to imprint designs or patterns into the steel.

The students were taught how to identify the different types of steel by spark tests and drill tests and how to temper mild steel with heat. The trick was to heat the object to a cherry red glow then immediately immerse it in oil until it cooled.

Toward the end of the course, Mr. Burbank announced that the students would now be required to put their newfound knowledge and skills to use and choose a steel item to create out of a block of mild steel. Michael decided to create a small mechanic's "breaker bar" wrench. The project turned out to be more complicated than he had expected, but it seemed that even the unflappable Mr. Burbank was somewhat taken with it. The finished wrench turned out to be nearly unidentifiable from a store-bought one of the same size, but Michael had not been able to perfect the tempering process of it to his satisfaction. He had not been aware that tool steel requires an extra, super-hard tempering process. Still, he was rather proud of his finished product, and he had the satisfaction of hearing a number of adults comment on the ingenuity of it.

Auto mechanics class was also fascinating and highly educational. The students spent countless hours learning how cars, trucks, and even tractors are made and how they function. They delved into the intricacies of carburetors, and each student had to bring a carburetor in and totally dismantle it and soak it in the cleaning acid then reassembled it with a new rebuild kit. Michael practiced on the family Chevy, and wonder of wonders, it worked when he was finished. Near the end of the course, their assignment was to completely overhaul a car, truck, or tractor motor. The only motor Michael had available was the tired old John Deere A on the farm. Carl was surprisingly open to having him overhaul it, so he pop-popped his way through town and checked it in for his project.

Over the next few months, he totally dismantled the engine, ground the valves, honed the cylinders, and installed a total rebuild kit. The shop floor was covered with cars and tractors being rebuilt by students, and at times they got into each other's spaces. One day, Michael was walking past a classmate who was attempting to start his Farmall tractor with a heavy iron crank. The tractor backfired at exactly the wrong instant, tearing the heavy crank from his hands and sending it crashing into Michael's skull. The pain was excruciating, but since there was no blood, it did not get checked out by medical personnel. He suffered for many years with excruciating headaches, but it was a time when you were expected to suck it up and keep going, so life went on. The seriousness of wounds was largely determined by the amount of blood that flowed, and his wound hadn't bled.

When the engine was totally overhauled and running smoothly, he sanded down the body and gave it a new paint job, then he wired it with new lights, installed a new seat, and the tractor looked and sounded like it had just rolled off the assembly line. His glow of satisfaction was dampened slightly when he got the bill for the new parts to take home to his father. The bill was over three hundred dollars (over two thousand dollars in 2020 dollars). Michael had had no idea that the cost of parts, and materials was adding up so fast, since the instructor had stressed that the school got a large discount on parts and materials which they passed on to the students. To his surprise, his parents paid it with very little criticism. It helped that the rusty clunker of a farm tractor was now a new restoration, but that was a lot of money which was not in the family budget.

# FINAL NAIL IN THE COFFIN

One afternoon, Michael was waiting on the front steps of the school for his mother to pick him up. There were several other students around him also waiting for rides, but his attention was on his conversation with Sherri Bannon. They were standing several feet apart chatting when Charlotte rolled up in the family car. Michael said goodbye to Sherri and climbed in the car to head home. He noticed that his mother seemed rather irritated but didn't think a lot about it. He assumed she was irritated because he had been talking with a despised Bannon. He really wished she could get over it, especially since she was so accomplished at working Carl up into one of his rages to accomplish her purposes. A close Raptor-Bannon relationship was absolutely *not* going to happen! She would see to this no matter what means necessary.

At home, Michael changed into his clothes for chores. At sixteen, he was starting to make up for his formerly slow growth, although he still had more catching up to do. He was in the horse barn when his father stalked in. Michael could see by the dark look on his face that his father was in a black mood. Although Charlotte had tried to infuriate him toward Michael, Carl was making an effort to control himself. "Come here," he commanded. "I need to talk to you."

Michael stopped what he had been doing and listened as his father told the story of his illegitimate birth then demanded that he totally break off communications with the Bannon girl so he didn't end up with the same consequences. Michael knew that their relationship had never been sexual in nature and was not headed there any time soon. He couldn't understand why, when there was absolutely no evidence of a physically inappropriate relationship with

Sherri, they would all but accuse him of having one. Their relationship had *never* been about that! But he listened silently right up to where his father began to demand a promise from him that he would never have anything to do with Sherri again. That was one thing he could definitely not promise, and the more he demurred, the angrier his father became until he was totally again controlled by the black rage.

"I know what you need!" he roared. "Drop your pants!"

Several thoughts crossed Michael's mind in mere seconds. The first was, *if I fight, he can take me anyway and might even kill me. I will drop my pants but* not *my shorts! And I will* not *scream or cry, no matter how bad it gets!*

Fortunately, Carl neglected to order him to drop his shorts this time. Seizing a length of harness leather, he began to swing viciously at his son's buttocks and bare legs. The pain from the blows was like the cut of hot knives, but he refused to make a sound. As the beating went on, he finally realized that his silence was only infuriating the monster more, and the severity of the blows was steadily increasing! He was hanging on to the barn wall to stay on his feet. Shocked realization hit him that he either had to start screaming and crying or this was going to end very badly. He began to scream and cry, and immediately the beating began to wind down. At least he was still on his feet, he realized, when the monster had been satiated.

"Now git up to your room until supper," his father grated. Michael pulled up his trousers, trying not to aggravate the fresh wounds, and with his self-respect shredded yet again, he walked out the barn door and headed for his room.

He had to lie face down on his cot because he could not lie on his bruised backside. Black thoughts began to consume him as he contemplated what had just happened. He despised himself for standing there and getting beaten like a mangy dog then feeding the beast with his agonized screams. *Was this ever going to stop? When?* He looked at his hunting rifle by the head of his bed. There was a handful of bullets on the nightstand, and he reached out and picked them up, his thoughts in a black swirl. *It would only take one bullet! Would he put the gun in his mouth or at his temple? Why did he have to be such a coward? He could have ended all this a long time ago!*

He was still turning these thoughts over in his mind when his father stalked in and ordered him downstairs for supper. The gun by the bed and bullets in his son's hand should have been a warning sign, but the god of the Raptor family never even noticed. What he did notice was that his son didn't jump fast enough when he called, so he strode to the bed and grabbed the hapless Michael by the shirt, hauled him off his cot, and shoved him toward the stairway. "When I call, you will come *immediately!*" he shouted, administering body blows on the way down the stairs. Supper was a silent affair, with Charlotte making artificial attempts at chatter but the boys silently eating then leaving the table.

The incident in the horse barn was the final nail in the coffin of any hope of a relationship between Michael and his father. There had been a brief period of time when Michael had been helping with the addition that his father had treated him like a person, but now it was obvious that he was again property. It would be decades later when Michael would finally learn that the evil deeds done by people are inspired by the enemy of their souls, and hatred toward the person of the evildoer is often misguided. As a boy trying to become a man, he could not see past the physical being dispensing the evil. The seeds of hatred and bitterness bloomed afresh toward his parents. He would reward them in kind whenever and wherever he found opportunity. He had learned in school about the passive resistance philosophies of great men like Mahatma Ghandi and Martin Luther King, but they made no sense to him at all! After all, their causes prevailed in the end, but they both ended up dead. If they were dead, how did they benefit from their sacrifices! He had also learned that the Bible teaches that the victors should enjoy their spoils or "winnings." He sometimes wondered how Carl Jr. felt about these things, but the brothers never discussed them.

When his folks had pressured Randy to leave for the summer to break up his relationship with Rene, Michael had written a heartfelt letter to his oldest brother and shared his frustrations with him. He got no response but found out later that Carl Jr. had written to

Randy and asked him about it, and he had just minimized it and sort of passed it off. Michael came to believe that he rationalized these incidents by telling himself that Michael probably deserved what he got. There was nowhere for Michael to turn to manage his internal demons. Once, he had tentatively tried to reach out to the high school counsellor in a rather vague way, but that guy had totally missed the cue as well. Nobody wanted to hear this stuff anyway, so he buried it, and life went on. He knew that his older brothers felt like he brought a lot of his troubles down on himself and recognized that they were probably at least partially right. But he hurt for them when they were mistreated and wondered why they didn't reciprocate. Someday, he decided, he would find and marry a woman who would understand him and love all the pain and heartache away! In years to come, he would be pretty sure God laughed out loud when he heard him come up with that plan! Indeed, he would himself marvel at his naïve stupidity of having believed that would be possible!

Meanwhile, he watched for opportunities to prove his own courage. If his parents were going to keep ratcheting up the pressure on his relationship with Miss Sherri, then he would double down on the relationship. An audacious plan began to form in his mind.

The next day in school, they again made opportunity to spend time together in an empty classroom.

"I need directions to your place," Michael told her, trying to sound casual. "I'm planning to come see you tonight."

"Oh, sure," she said dryly. "That's gonna happen."

"I'm serious," Michael said. "I have it all planned out. I just need to know how to get there!"

Sherri looked at him and saw the determination in his eyes. "How are you gonna do that?" she asked, the doubt clear in her voice. "It must be about ten or twelve miles!"

"I will ride our fastest horse," Michael replied, "and sneak out when everybody is asleep and back in before they wake up."

Sherri pondered the idea for a few minutes then slowly shook her head as she processed the ramifications of his crazy plan. "You're not going to come," she said dismissively.

That evening, Michael made sure Dusty was close to the barn, and his saddle and bridle were easily accessible. When it was bedtime, he took off his shoes and crawled into bed fully dressed. His adrenalin was pumping, keeping him on high alert as he listened to be sure everyone was in bed and sleeping. He would have to walk directly past his parent's bedroom located at the head of the stairs. He had carefully checked the entire stairway for creaky steps and memorized the danger areas. He knew that if he got caught, he could make up a cover story about wanting to go out and spend time with the horses, and there was an element of truth to that. He had shared his plan with no one, so there was no danger that one of his brothers had ratted him out, although that rarely happened, especially among the older boys.

A few minutes later, he was at the front door, wishing he had thought of oiling the hinges before bedtime. But good fortune was still smiling on him, and he was able to pass soundlessly out into the welcoming shadows.

Dusty eyed him suspiciously as Michael caught him and saddled him for the night's adventure. Michael led him down the lane past the house then mounted him when he reached the gravel road. When they were safely away from the farm, Michael lifted him into a stiff, ground-eating gallop. There was a partial moon dimly illuminating the road, but occasionally clouds would drift across it making the darkness complete. Michael began to worry a bit about his need to skirt the edge of Smithville. He would need to ride approximately six miles on the shoulder of a state road and ride through one traffic light. If a highway patrol car happened to see him, he would be investigated, and things would get very bad real fast! There was no cover story he could invent if he was caught this far from home and headed toward the Bannon's home!

As he rode into the outskirts of Smithville, Michael decided he would ride through at a stiff canter. The first glitch of the night's adventure suddenly appeared when Dusty made a parallel decision that he would go through Smithville at a leisurely walk. Michael felt a touch of panic when the horse absolutely refused to run. Michael never carried a whip when he rode, but his heels drummed a rhythm on Dusty's ribs, and he began to smack the end of the bridle reins across his rebellious rump, but the horse maintained his casual walk through the most risky part of the journey!

After what seemed like a very tense eternity, they finally reached the shadows on the far edge of town, and the buckskin decided he could cooperate and run again. Michael thought back to his half-wild Indian pony "Pal" he had ridden so long on the Reservation and wished he would be riding him now. Pal had been fearless and loved to run. He would undoubtedly have shaved at least an hour off this midnight ride.

Sherri's directions were good, and a few miles later, Michael turned into their long, tree-lined driveway. The trees were huge and thick, making the road so dark Dusty had to guide himself part of the way. They finally broke into a clearing, and there, dark and brooding, was the Bannon residence. Michael would have liked to see Sherri and delivered his I-told-you-so in person, but he was becoming concerned about the passing of time and his need to get back home before his father, a notoriously early riser, was up and about. He spied several fifty-five-gallon drums and dismounted and placed a note he had prepared for her on one of the drums and weighted it down with a stone. Then with a real feeling of accomplishment, he swung up on the recalcitrant buckskin and headed back down the dark spooky lane toward the road home.

The ride home was much the same as the ride out, but Michael was getting weary from the stress and beating the stubborn horse. When he approached Smithville again, he managed to coax the horse into an unenthused trot but no more. He didn't breathe easy until they were on the gravel road to their farm. He could only hope that the horse wouldn't begin to whinny and nicker with the other horses at the barn when he passed the house, but apparently the buckskin was as tired as he was.

At the barn, Michael slid stiffly from the saddle and removed the riding tack from the horse and turned him out to pasture. He hoped he would be far enough out that his father would not see him and notice the signs of his hard night's ride. He removed his shoes as he approached the front door. This would be about the riskiest time of all, he realized. He would have to sneak all the way through the house and up the stairs when the first streaks of dawn were lighting the sky, and everyone had had a night's sleep rather than when they had lain their tired bodies down the preceding night to enjoy their first deep sleep of the night. He stole into his room without waking his brother who shared the room and was asleep minutes after he hit the mattress.

It seemed only a few minutes later when his unsuspecting mother was waking him to begin the new day. He had pulled it off! He couldn't wait to tell Miss Bannon that he had been to her place in the dead of night. He decided he would just mention it casually like it had been no big deal. When he broke it to her, Sherri absolutely did not believe him! Trying to maintain a cool-dude nonchalance, Michael began to describe their place in as much detail as the night shadows had allowed him to observe. He could see the wheels of her mind turning as she said, "Have you been to our place before?"

"Nope," he replied, "why do you think I had to ask you for directions yesterday? But if you don't believe me, I left you a note under a stone on one of those barrels out front."

"Okay, I'll look when I get home," she responded. The next day, she brought the note to school. Michael had made a believer out of her. He knew he had a lot to learn until his rough edges from their crude upbringing were smoothed out, but courage and achievement was something her family respected.

# FIVE MINUTES TO TWELVE

"Well, I have some news," Charlotte announced on evening at the supper table. "We are going to get some company." She went on to detail her telephone conversation with Jeanie, her niece from Kentucky. Jeanie was Aunt Olivia and Uncle Laverne's daughter. While she was not as flamboyant and outgoing as her older brother Henry, the Raptor boys had had a lot of great times with her when they had attended the same church. But she had fallen hard for a super nice and decent young man from their neighboring state, and they had been married for a couple years now. Her husband Steve and she had decided to buy an RV and spend an entire year on the road touring the country and visiting relatives and friends. They would be stopping overnight at the Raptors on their journey. Their visit would have ramifications beyond catching up socially.

Randy and Steve hit it off well, and Steve mentioned that there was a feed mill near them that was looking for help, and they had an extra room in their house where Randy could board with them if he was interested in moving. Randy was very interested in moving there, but there was one very large glitch. His relationship with Rene, which once had been rock solid, was beginning to fracture from the stresses.

There was trouble brewing in the formerly happy and peaceful Glendale church, and once again Carl and Charlotte Raptor were smack in the middle of it. It had begun when some of the older boys were summoned to Selective Service by Uncle Sam. The Mennonites profess to be a non-resistant faith and as such were allowed to perform an alternate service to the military draft. The young fellows who left were many miles away from their parents and learned much about the world outside their customary Mennonite restraints. Social trends such as shaggy or long hair for guys began to show up when these young men returned home for their brief visits and a few families in the church were becoming very upset.

The ever-popular Leon Kurtz seemed to draw the most fire. He had an outgoing personality that made younger guys want to emulate him, and he wasn't particularly concerned about how people thought he should live his life. When he showed up in church with hair over the tops of his ears, the unified spirit of the congregation began to fracture. Uncle Laverne's joined with Carl and Charlotte in pressuring Pastor Lowell to make rules against these things creeping into the church. There were meetings public and private which led to criticism, accusations, and condemnations. Some of the families were okay with letting these things run their course, but those who objected were having none of it!

As the adults began to criticize and condemn each other, the young people were caught in the middle. The formerly harmonious church services began to become times of discord and tension. Once, when Carl was in front of the group presenting a devotional meditation, his emotions overcame him, and he stopped speaking for a few moments. When he spoke again, his voice was pitched high with stress, and his face was twitching uncontrollably.

"I have seen God's clock!" he said forcefully. "And it was five minutes to twelve! I shudder to think what time it is now!"

Michael never doubted what his father shared that day. He also had no doubt about when he had seen it! Carl had seen many incredible things as a prophet in the little South Dakota chapel when it had been shaken by a radical revival sixteen years ago. He had been one of a few who had received the gift of prophesy and had seen his prophesies come to pass in miraculous ways. But the Mennonite bishops could not allow one of their congregations to continue down an unknown path, claiming the Holy Spirit was in control, which would be a threat to their control.

Their solution was to demand that every member of the congregation who had been involved in the revival must stand before the church body and confess that this had all been from Satan. The pastor and several of the younger men absolutely refused because they didn't believe it, and such a proclamation would expose them to the very real danger of committing the unforgivable sin according to Matthew 12:24–32 and Luke 12:9–10. But most of the group bowed to the pressure and stood to attribute it to Satan.

What his father shared that morning would haunt Michael to some degree all his adult life. *If his father believed that he had seen God's clock, then there was no way he could have believed that Satan had been in charge of the revival! Satan has no power to show someone God's clock! And if his father had known the revival was from the Holy Spirit and stood to claim it was from Satan, that was a direct violation of what Jesus had powerfully warned the religious folks about in Matthew 12! But believed that his father was a Christian for all his weaknesses, so he would let it go and let God sort it out.*

As the Glendale church situation deteriorated, Carl's and Laverne's began to seriously consider transferring their membership to the strict conservative Clayton church. No one caught the irony that the nonresistant professing Mennonite congregation was fighting and headed for a split over the young men they had sent to alternate service because they professed nonresistance. The fighting and unpleasantness continued.

One night, Pastor Lowell and his wife came to the Raptor home to discuss the situation with Carl and Charlotte. Several of the Raptor boys' ears were glued to the heat vent between the living room and their bedroom as the conversation unfolded. Carl and Charlotte were rigid and even snide as the gentle pastor pleaded with them not to destroy the unity of the church. There was no middle ground found, and by the end of the conversation, the boys knew that their happy days of Glendale church were over.

Caught directly in the middle were Randy and Rene. They were not old enough to get married and found their families on opposite sides of the battles. Charlotte had determined that their relationship was not a good match, and Carl agreed. They had been pressuring Randy to break it off and stress cracks were widening in the relationship. Now this proposal from Steve and Jeannie seemed like a gift from Heaven. When their year-long tour was over, Randy had decided to accept the offer and move out to live with them. Miss Rene handled her heartbreak with admirable decorum, and the Raptors began to attend the Clayton church.

This was the beginning of religious dynamics the likes of which Michael had never seen. But as always, the Raptor boys had no vote; they went where they were told. For the rest of his life, Michael would strongly maintain that the few years they had spent attending the Glendale church were the best church experience of his life. He was now headed straight into an unpleasant church experience. But he had lots of cousins there to help him navigate the new religious dynamics.

The Sunday services at the Clayton church always followed the same format. A designated man would rise and open the service with two hymns from one of the two hymnals. There were absolutely no musical instruments of any type allowed in the church. After the songs, a man who had been chosen to serve for a year as Sunday school superintendent would go to the front to present a brief devotional. There was a special lectern on the floor directly in front of the pulpit for those of lesser ecclesiastical stature than the esteemed ordained men to make their assigned presentations. The Sunday school superintendent would then dismiss the classes to their designated locations with their duly elected teachers. Only the very youngest classes were allowed to be taught by women, who were strictly admonished to remain silent in the church. This was based on the scriptures like 1 Timothy 2:12 and 1 Corinthians 14:35.

There was one of the elderly women in church however, who made up for the mandatory female silence during the congregational singing. On certain songs, her shrill, slightly quivering voice would rise above the throng and kind of hang in the air above the congregation. It reminded Michael of the sound effects resulting from the altercations between their two tomcats at full throated fury!

In time, Rene met and married a handsome and solid young man, and Randy would maintain that she was fortunate life worked out the way it had. Many years later in the same community, the family would lay Carl Raptor to rest on Michael's forty-second birthday. There was no birthday celebration, given the sadness of the occasion, but Michael was deeply moved afterward when Rene brought him a birthday cake.

"I know it is a sad day for you," she said, "but it *is* your birthday!"

Michael was astounded by her act of kindness! She had remembered his birthday after all these years and after all the heartache! Then she had had the courage to bring him a cake at such a time! It was a kindness he would never forget!

Church life at the Clayton church was similar in many ways but very different in others. It was Michael's first exposure to the conservative Mennonite system where the leadership exercises complete control of all aspects of religious life as well as most aspects of everyday life. The Clayton church took the opposite approach to leadership as the Glendale congregation in that their policy was to have many ordained men in the ministry who made decisions concerning what would and would not be allowed and announced them to the congregants. In the past, they had fought over such things as requiring the women to wear black nylon stockings, requiring the black hats to be worn, and allowing members to listen to the radio. The use of television was so wicked that no one seriously even considered trying to use TV. Young people and even some of the older folks were often embarrassingly eager to watch TV, and it would draw them like a magnet whenever they were in a home or store where a TV was turned on.

Bishop Neil Wagner was a rather quiet and austere man who was married to Charlotte's oldest sister. He took his religion and church responsibilities very seriously and was not a man to be pushed around or persuaded contrary to his beliefs. He appeared to be a good father and raised a large family of respectable children. Several of his sons would eventually be ordained as ministers, bishops, and deacons, and at least one of them would become a good bit more radically conservative than Neill himself.

Bishop Neil had clashed with Charlotte's youngest brother Harold Reynolds on the church related issues. While Harold was also very conservative in many areas, he didn't see a lot of value in requiring the women to wear black stockings, especially when that was what the "ladies of the night" were known for. He also felt the radio could be useful, but the church leaders had decreed that all radio antennae on vehicles must be removed. More than one of the young fellows carried a piece of stiff, heavy wire under their front seats to stick in the socket where the antenna had been when there was no one to see them. Although Harold would deny it to his dying day, the rumor was that he had solved the problem by leaving his radio antenna intact and simply draping a black nylon stocking over it when they went to church.

Michael never knew if Uncle Harold had actually done this or not, but there was an antenna standing tall on the family van, and one Sunday night when he had spent the day with his cousin at their house, the kids piled into the van to head for church. The oldest boy was driving, and there were no adults in the vehicle. As they were about to drive out the lane, one of the boys said, "Hey, wait, you forgot the black stocking" wherewith one of the boys ran into the house and returned with a black nylon stocking which they draped over the antenna, after which they drove to church. It was obviously not the first time they had pulled of that maneuver to "sanctify" the radio antenna. Bishop Neil and others of his persuasion saw this practice as a poke in the eye, but Uncle Harold was intelligent and so well-versed in Bible knowledge that it was nearly impossible for anyone to come out the victor in an argument with him. Once, a brother in the church was lamenting to one of the ministers about a grievance he had with Harold, and the minister advised him to go and talk it out with Harold as Jesus had instructed in the book of Matthew chapter 18.

The aggrieved brother looked at the minister like he had lost his mind and said, "Oh no! Every time I approach him about something, I end up having to make a confession before the church!"

One of the preachers' favorite drums to beat was men's hair they considered too long for professing Christians. Their dry and uninspiring sermons were often laced with harangues about the evil of too long hair on men and the horrific evil of women cutting their hair. Conservative Mennonite girls' and women's hair was not to be cut or even trimmed between birth and death. The cutting of women's hair was not much of an issue though. It was so egregious an act that the line was rarely even approached, much less crossed. The young guys, though, were a different story. It was easy to put off the haircuts until the hair got shaggy and began to cover the tops of the ears. The church had a long, multipage handbook of rules spelling out in detail what was allowed and what was forbidden. In addition to the rule against long or shaggy hair, the rules said that men shall have no outlandish hair. The rules were also spelled out in detail as to how the girls' and women's hair was to be braided or put up.

The proverbial axe was usually applied to the root of perceived church rule infractions when the biannual church communion time came along, The church leaders would announce the upcoming "preparatory service" at which the leaders would assemble in a separate room to "receive members' counsel and testimonies to their own state of spiritual purity. The council meetings often ended up being times when the congregation underwent a course adjustment to get them back on the straight and narrow way. Members' frustrations and irritations toward other members they felt were not keeping the letter of the law got aired in the privacy of the counsel room with the all-powerful ministers. These events had little in common with the somber and reflective last supper where Jesus instructed his followers to focus on the sacrifice of his blood and body to redeem lost and fallen men!

In properly administrated churches, the instructions of Jesus from Matthew chapter 18 are followed, where members are instructed to approach each other kindly with a humble spirit and share their concerns. This, however, required courage most members seemed not to possess. As in the case with Harold, the person being approached would often react with anger, self-justification, etc. It was much easier just to tattle to the preachers and let them crack the whip. Most of them seemed to enjoy it anyway! The dynamic which was especially problematic was when members allowed an irritation to fester until they became angry enough that their anger gave them a type of false courage to take the offending member to task. But by now, they were so upset that there would be no kindness or humility in their approach, and they would rip into them verbally. This would immediately put the perceived offender on the defensive whereby he or she would catalogue the faults of the approaching member right back at them, setting up the perfect setting for an ongoing fight.

Thus, the coming of communion tended to be a time to be dreaded by many of the youth and anticipated by the more critical members. The real purpose of communion observance—the sober, deeply grateful remembrance of the sacrifice of God's Son to buy mankind's salvation—was usually tainted or even overshadowed by criticisms and strife over things like whose hair was too long and who was not dressing conservatively enough, etc.

Whether the system was ideal or not, it was what they had and very similar to what most conservative Mennonite churches had. People learned from childhood on up to fit in and make it work. There were many sincere, God-fearing members in these congregations. However, it was a religious order that was virtually impossible to sell the people who had not been raised in it. There were occasional families who were interested enough to try to join with them, but almost without exception, they all moved on. Some of their marriage-age children married Mennonites and stayed with the church, but there were not many of them either.

There was, however, a lot of good in the Mennonite culture, which was in large part what attracted the outside people who did attempt to join. Destructive practices such as drug use, alcoholism, free sex, tobacco, gambling, etc. were not allowed, and although there were incidents where members fell into some of these vices, they were required to repent, confess, and forsake them if they wished to continue in the membership.

They also stressed decent, common family living where the fathers stayed with their families and took their responsibilities seriously. The fact that dark and evil secrets were covered up in some homes did not negate the value of what the Mennonites were trying to achieve. Even most of those who left the Mennonite culture would carry a lasting appreciation for the overall good they had been raised with. The ones scarred by physical and sexual abuse within the religious order found it more difficult. Some of these, however, stayed with the religion and continued the cycle of abuse behind closed doors.

Some of the married men seemed to try to out-conservative each other. When it came to the shortest hair, most of the young fellows agreed that Michael's former boss Shem Skinner, who had been ordained as a deacon, took the prize. In a style that would one day be fashionable, the sides of his head were nearly shaved to the skin with a short mop of hair left on top. It was rather amusing to the young guys when he came to church with a fresh haircut. The white skin around the sides and back of his head shone pale white, contrasting sharply with the deep "farmer's tan" of his face and neck.

Most of the young men would try to be sure their hair was acceptably short in the weeks leading up to the preparatory service. But there was one family who didn't get real invested in what others thought of them. They had two teenage sons named Grant and Justin. Grant, the eldest son, was singled out in the council room on one occasion for a tongue-lashing by the bishop.

"It has been noted," he began, "that you always seem to keep your hair too long. We want you to promise to do better at keeping it short!"

Grant looked at him, somewhat surprised, as though no one had mentioned this to him before. "Yeah," he replied, "I can do that. I'm not trying to give you guys a hassle or anything!"

"There won't be any hassle!" the bishop retorted. "You will keep it short or you will be out of the fellowship!"

Grant, who had an easygoing personality, left the meeting smarting from the rough rebuke. "They ought to look in the mirror," he fumed to Michael. "The standards clearly say, 'no outlandish haircuts.' You tell me that Shem's haircut is not outlandish!"

Michael enjoyed hanging out with some of his cousins his age, but many of the youth activities were a real bust. Where they had been loved and appreciated in the Glendale youth group, he had the strong impression that he was looked down on by many of these youth. They tended to be blunt and discourteous to each other, saying anything and everything that went through their minds. Randy fit in better and was more appreciated as he began adopting and espousing their very conservative speech and practices. He would follow the unquestioning conservative path while Michael had too many questions and could not just gloss over the inconsistencies. He joined the church and his parents made sure he kept his hair short as he managed to fit in...mostly. Life was rapidly becoming more fluid as the months passed.

# THE WEDDING

Carl Jr. was settling down and getting married. He had met a quiet, soft-spoken girl named Linda, and they had been dating long enough that they were ready to tie the proverbial knot. Carl Jr. was now a job foreman and doing well financially. He was driving a plush new Ford LTD, and her parents, who were co-owners of a large family farming enterprise, had a house for them to rent. The 1966 Malibu had been sold back to his father and was being used as the family car. The plan was for the remaining family to load all his remaining possessions and wedding gifts in an enclosed trailer and tow it out with the Malibu. It seemed like a solid plan—except for the fact that the trailer Carl bought was a flat deck with neither sides nor roof.

"Not a problem," he happily assured them, "I will just build the walls and roof with plywood.

*Oh, sweet!* Michael thought. *I'll bet that's gonna be a doozy!*

When it was finished, Michael had to admit that it didn't look too bad. The unpainted plywood looked much better than the garish gold paint he had splashed on the top carrier box for the Alaska trip. When it was loaded, Carl decided to repack the bearings with axel grease. "They had the bearings way too tight," he remarked to Michael, "so I loosened them up when I put them back together." Since his mechanical training had not covered axels and bearings, Michael didn't think much about the remark.

They pulled out early in the morning, and when daylight finally overtook them, Michael looked back at the trailer and noticed one of the wheels was flopping badly. He brought the problem to Carl's attention, despite the fact that he was extremely irritated that his mother had instructed his father not to allow him to drive. It would have been easier to take if she had just told him upfront that he was not going to be allowed to drive on the trip instead of just rebuffing his requests to drive the whole trip. Carl did not enjoy driving, and Michael knew he would have been happy to let him take over, but Charlotte was particularly irritated with her middle son the last while, and this was a very good opportunity to make him pay for whatever transgressions she held against him.

They unhitched the trailer beside the road, and Carl pulled out the ruined bearings which he had so carefully packed. They found an auto parts store in the next town, and he bought new bearings and more grease then returned to the trailer to reassemble it. He was careful to allow plenty of play in it again when he finished the assembly. A couple hours later, they were back on the road to the wedding.

They had been driving about forty-five minutes when Michael noticed that the wheel on the other side was flopping. They pulled over again, unhitched the trailer, and went in search of bearings. This time, they were difficult to locate, and Carl needed the visit several stores until he located them. By now, he was getting wise to the situation and purchased an extra set of bearings. They returned to the trailer, replaced the bearings, and headed out again.

A couple hours further down the road, Michael announced that the first wheel was flopping again. Carl was getting frustrated, so Michael got more involved in the replacement project. "I think you might be leaving them too loose," he commented. Carl was out of ideas, so he allowed Michael to snug the bearings like they had been originally. Then he jacked up the other side of the trailer and snugged that bearing as well. He really didn't know if this was the right thing to do, but he knew they had to do something different. It worked! They had no more bearing problems. But before this trip ended, they would know what real mechanical problems were!

They swung by to pick up Randy in Kentucky and take him along out to the wedding. They spent the night with Steve and Jeannie then headed back east early the next morning. From here on, Randy would do all the driving. He tried to give Michael a chance to drive, but Charlotte would have none of it. They all knew it had nothing to do with his driving ability, it was just a good opportunity for him to pay for whatever sins had his mother upset with him.

The trip was immediately more fun with Randy along. Michael had always gotten along a little better with him and didn't envy his "good boy" standing. His older brothers each had things going for them that he didn't have. Carl Jr. had been the indispensable big boy who was the most valuable helper around the home and farm. Randy was the one who tried hardest to please, with a fair measure of success. Michael's only claim to fame was that he was good with horses. That came in handy at some levels but was a rather worthless way to garner brownie points. Johnny would later claim that he had lived in the shadows of all three, but he also got along reasonably well at home while the older boys were still there. Eli was just busy being the typical baby of the family.

Carl was extremely vigilant about checking the motor oil. He had brought some extra quarts with him, knowing the car was using some. "It's good to keep your engine oil a quart over full," he informed his boys. "I read that in an article written by a car expert."

After the bearings fiasco, Michael couldn't let that one pass. His father was getting bad mechanical information, and he needed to rescue him!

"Mr. Marconi says just the opposite," he said. "He says that you could blow your engine by overfilling the oil."

"How would that blow an engine?" Carl asked.

"He says the crankshaft can hit the oil and either whip it into a foam or throw it up onto the hot pistons and blow them," Michael said. He and Randy were in total agreement that Mr. Marconi's word was final.

Their father remained unconvinced and continued to keep the oil level a quart over full.

As they entered Pennsylvania, the terrain became mountainous and the scenery beautiful. From the turnpike, the secondary roads became smaller and more winding. The uphill and downhill grades became gradually steeper as they drove. There was a lot of stone-work—on buildings, fences, and bridges.

They arrived at Grandpa Raptors late that night, tired and sore. Grandpa's lived in an old but well-maintained stone house that was three stories tall but not real large on each floor. After one of Grandma's big suppers, the boys climbed two flights of stairs to reach the upstairs bedrooms, where they were soon fast asleep.

The next day, they hauled the trailer load of Carl Jr.'s possessions to the house where they would be living. It was another tall stone house nestled in a valley with a pond nearby. The water supply from the house came from a spring higher up the mountain. The spring was high enough and strong enough that there was no need for a pressure pump. They simply piped it directly into the house plumbing.

They were discussing the trip as they unloaded the trailer, and Randy mentioned that he had driven all day. "Why didn't you let Michael help with the driving?" Carl Jr. asked, looking at his parents. Charlotte smiled her tight, plastic banana smile and said, "We prefer Randy's driving." Her tone left no doubt that the subject was closed.

Michael never knew if that episode had anything to do with his big brother asking him to chauffer them from the wedding ceremony to the photographers then to the reception, but driving the snazzy new LTD made up for being stiffed on the family trip.

This being the first wedding in the family made it extra special. There was the last-minute flurry of activity getting the reception area set up and making sure all the details were covered for the ceremony. When the wedding ceremony was over, Carl Jr. and Linda climbed into the backseat of the LTD, and Michael pulled away from the church. He tried not to look into the rearview mirror so they could smooch in peace, but he had to chuckle at the first comment his brother made to his new bride.

"Well," he said, "now we are man and wife for the rest of our life!"

After the wedding pictures were taken, they headed back to the reception for the celebration feast. The festivities were fun, after which the family went to Linda's parents' house to see the couple off on their honeymoon. When the taillights of the LTD faded into the night, Michael felt a mild sense of loss. Somehow this made it all final that Carl Jr. was gone for good.

The Raptors stayed for the rest of the weekend then headed out Monday morning, towing the empty trailer. Randy was driving, and Michael and Johnny were in the front seat with him. The first sign of trouble came several hours into the trip. They were cruising down the interstate when smoke began to drift out of the tailpipe. The car gradually began to lose power as the smoke increased from a wisp to a billowing cloud. The engine began to misfire and it was obvious that they could not go on like this.

The tension was increasing rapidly in the Malibu. Finally, Carl spoke, his voice charged to the breaking point from the stress. "Randy," he said, "pull over."

Randy pulled the car and trailer over on the shoulder and switched off the motor. They sat for a few minutes in total stress-charged silence, no one looking at anyone else. Then Carl spoke again.

"Boys," he said, his voice trembling with emotion, "take off your hats!"

Michael was a bit surprised at this instruction. Apparently, they were going to pray! They had prayers before meals and the evenings when they had family devotions, but he had never heard a prayer offered when they actually needed something!

The boys took off their hats and bowed their heads, waiting for the prayer. Long moments passed in absolute silence. Suddenly Carl burst out in loud, racking sobs! It wasn't actually a prayer, at least not in any kind of normal format. He just sobbed out loud and said, "What are we gonna do?" a couple times then fell silent. After a period of silence, Randy and Michael looked across at each other. They both realized that it was going to be up to them to work toward a solution. They climbed out and raised the hood, but everything looked intact with the engine.

After some discussion, they decided they would have to walk to the next emergency call box on the freeway. They were not sure if they were closer to the one behind them or the one ahead. They decided to walk forward. They walked and ran for several miles until they finally saw the welcome emergency phone box ahead. Now if they could just manage to reach someone who was at home. They knew all their relatives and acquaintances would be starting their busy weeks but were hoping they could reach someone who hadn't yet left home.

Randy dialed the number for Grandpa's and was hugely relieved to hear Grandma answer the phone. He explained their situation to her and Grandpa and gave them their approximate location, and they promised to send help. With a sense of relief and accomplishment, Michael and Randy hiked back to the stranded car and reported their success.

The wait for help seemed endless, but finally a green Ford pickup with a handmade bed topper pulled up behind them. It was Pastor Randy, their old missionary pastor from the South Dakota reservation. He soon had the hood raised and began to pull off spark plug wires one at a time to determine which cylinder had the problem. He traced the problem to the rear cylinder, and when he unplugged the spark plug wire, the smoking stopped, and the motor ran smoother. "Okay," he said, "if you go to the next turnaround and head back, I will follow you back to where we can fix it."

They arrived back at Grandpa's without further incident, and Carl's brother John offered them the use of his basement garage.

Next morning, they pulled the car into his garage and began to tear the motor apart.

Uncle John helped with the project, and kept the boys entertained with his jokes and stories.

The real professional, though, was pastor Randy. In his slow, quiet way, he directed each step of the project until they had dug down to the bowels of the engine. The problem was self-evident when they peered down into the rear cylinder. The overfilled crankcase oil had apparently been picked up by the crankshaft and thrown up into the rear cylinder, blowing a hole in it. They speculated that the steep Pennsylvania hills may have aggravated the overfilled crankcase. Michael didn't dare mention it, but it was indisputable proof that Mr. Marconi had been right.

A couple days later, the car was repaired, and they headed west again. They arrived in Kentucky to drop Randy off, and when he opened the hood to show Steve the repaired motor, he was shocked to discover that the spark plug wire was disconnected, and the repaired cylinder had not been used the whole way back. If they had known, they could have disconnected it at the first sign of trouble and drove it home with the same result!

There was some discussion about Randy moving back home, and Michael was really hoping he would. There was an attractive, dark-haired girl named Maria from the Birchwood church that had caught his interest, and he was seriously considering getting to know her better. He decided to wrap things up and move back home soon.

# BIRCHWOOD BUDDIES
# AND CARS

One of the positive things that came out of the church change was their interaction with the Birchwood youth group. Nathan, the scrawny blond kid he had met in the pickup truck, was a part of that youth group, and he continued to be friendly. There were several others about his age in that group as well, and in time, they began to be friends. Nathan, who by now was called Nate, felt the way Michael very much did about all the church rules, so they had some big things in common right away. He had some friends about his age that lived in the area who attended a liberal church with their permissive parents. The boys, Wilber Friedman, who was seventeen, and his sixteen-year-old brother Johnny, had their own cars and knew how to party. They didn't come to the Birchwood youth activities, but Nate found occasions to invite Michael to his house, and they slipped away to hang out with them. There was another guy their age from the Birchwood church who hung out with them occasionally too. His name was Lane Friedman, but he was not a close relative of the other Friedman boys. He had a dry sense of humor and a ready, infectious laugh and was fun to be around. Unlike Nate and Michael, Lane got along reasonably well with his father.

Nate and Michael were all about cars and looking forward to buying their first cars. Michael had ended up buying the 1966 Malibu which had been passed around the family. By now, the engine was so bad it was barely drivable, but with his mechanics training, he was sure he could fix it. A major engine overhaul was a daunting prospect, though, and he was trying to find time to get it done. One day, he was nosing around a junkyard when he spotted a 1955 Chevy. The body was badly rusted, but the salvage yard owner said the engine ran fine so Michael paid him a couple hundred dollars for it and drove it home. He was pretty sure the 283 cubic inch motor in it would fit in the Malibu, so his plan was to swap engines and junk the '55 again. As he got to comparing motors though, it looked to him like it would not work after all, so he started driving the junker around.

One evening, he got a call from Nate. He was all enthused about the Nova Super Sport he had just bought and said, "I heard you have a car too, why don't you bring it up for the weekend?"

"My car needs a motor," Michael said, "It's not drivable yet."

"But you have another car, don't you?" his friend persisted.

"Well, just this old junker," Michael replied. He hadn't really thought of it as a car, just a way to get around.

"Well, bring it up," Nate said, "we'll have some fun."

The rest of the week, Michael spent all his spare time patching rust holes in the old Chevy. He lifted the mats on the floor and laid plywood over the rust holes. Then he changed the oil and filled it with gas. Friday afternoon when he got off work, he headed for Birchwood.

When he arrived at Nate's house, he felt rather foolish pulling up in the huge old rusty Chevy. But Nate didn't seem to notice as he eagerly showed him his gleaming blue Nova SS with the black stripes. They climbed in and headed over to pick up Wilbur and Johnnie.

They drove the twelve miles to Birchwood in Nate's Super Sport and cruised around town. Michael had never cruised town just for sport. As children at home, they had occasionally been allowed to accompany one of their parents to town but were usually ordered to sit in the car while the parents shopped. Since trips to town had been infrequent when they lived on the reservation, shopping took quite long, and for the barefoot boys in the often sweltering, sometimes freezing parked car, the waits seemed endless. In spite of that inconvenient dynamic, they still never missed an opportunity to go along to town.

After about an hour of cruising town, Nate pulled the Blue Nova up to the root beer stand where they ordered soft drinks and appreciated the female serving staff. When it was time to move on, they cruised some more then headed back for the night. It was heady stuff for Michael to hang with his buddies without his parents" nagging control. The weekend passed too quickly, and Sunday night he drove back home to sleep. Thinking over the fun of the weekend, he realized that he needed to get a cool car. Since he had given up on rebuilding the Malibu, he started looking around for options.

The solution to his car need came up fast out of left field. Uncle Don heard that he was looking for a car and offered to sell him his 1968 Mustang. It was in showroom condition—light green with a black vinyl roof. He claimed that the motor had been factory re-bored for more power, and Michael had only to drive it to believe him.

There was one big obstacle to his purchasing the car. Although Uncle Don had offered it at a very good price, it was still more money than he could scrape together. Randy, always a better mechanic than Michael, had been examining the '55 Chevy motor a bit more closely and was pretty sure he could fit it in the Malibu, so he bought both cars from Michael.

It was becoming obvious, however, that Michael would have to borrow some money. Since he had no credit established, a bank loan would require his father to cosign. To his surprise, Carl agreed to go with him to get a bank loan. The banker readily approved the loan, and soon the Mustang was his. It drove like a dream and had some extra features such as cruise control and air conditioning. It got good mileage in spite of the modified engine. Michael loved the car, and Uncle Don was pleased that he had ended up with it.

The logging job had not been very satisfactory, mostly because of several rubber paychecks that had to be massaged into validity. Michael had been working near Randy one day when some brush kicked his chainsaw at full throttle, back and gashed his knee. There was a huge four-inch gash across his left knee, and he held it together with his fingers as Randy helped him hobble through the tall grass to his car for the trip to the doctor's office. Cleaning the wound was painful because grass seeds had gotten into the large open area, and they had to be fished and scrubbed out. For some reason, the doctor had him lying on the table with his right leg hanging down while he worked on the left leg's wound. When it was clean, he instructed Michael to raise the right leg to the table beside the left leg. Lying prone, Michael could not see the tray that the nurse had positioned directly over his right leg, and when it came up, his work boot smashed into the tray, and a shower of instruments went flying in all directions. The doctor was noticeably irritated, but there was nothing to be done except clean up the mess.

When it was cleaned up, the doctor prepared to sew the wound shut. He pumped a local anesthetic around the edges of the wound then began to stitch. For some reason, he had not numbed the last inch of the wound and each stitch toward the end became more painful. By the time he got to the last two stitches, Michael felt the needle pierce the flesh, felt the sutures being dragged through the needle hole, and felt when he pulled it tight and tied the knot. He was never quite sure if the doctor's failure to numb the end of the wound was sloppy work or payback for the kicked tray mess!

Michael had eventually taken the job at the feed mill Randy had left to move out to Steve's. He knew it was a physically demanding job and was hoping it would help him build upper body strength like it had his brother. The mill foreman was still his cousin Paul Manning who had lived across the road from Doug Bylers when he had worked there. But now Paul's had sold their small farm and bought a house in the village directly across from the feed mill. Paul was about six years older than Michael and was good friends with Cousin Henry. Henry's had left the Mennonite church years before, and Paul's were considering doing the same. Michael and Paul had many interesting chats on this and other subjects, but Michael felt quite strongly that his cousin disrespected him. But he was a reasonably good boss, and the starting pay was a whopping $2.25 per hour.

The work was the toughest Michael had ever done. The feed mill was combined with a lumber and building company, and the owner was a tight-fisted millionaire who refused to spend money to modernize. In spite of the fact that they had a railroad spur into their yard that brought in a steady stream of boxcars full of lumber and feed aggregates, the place owned neither forklift nor front loader. Every plank of lumber was unloaded and stacked by hand, and every pound of feed aggregate was unloaded with a scoop shovel. When a new boxcar load of aggregate was there in the morning, Michael knew exactly how his day was going to go. If it was loaded with lumber, one of the pole barn building crews would stay in from the job to help unload it. The boxcars were stacked almost completely to the roof, and four or five men would crawl in on top of the tons of planks and building materials and hand it out the sliding door to the rest of the crew outside. They would carry the lumber to the proper bins in the lumber yard. The process could take most of the day or less depending on how many employees were assigned to the project. It was hard physical work and extremely hot in the summer and bitterly cold in the winter.

One hot summer morning, Michael was assigned to assist a building crew in unloading a carload of lumber that had arrived the preceding night. The foreman had opened the sliding side door and climbed most of the way to the top of the load when an unstable stack of planks collapsed directly onto his leg and foot. His instant agonized screams were awful to hear! For the first few moments, the rest of the crew stood stunned! Then there was a swarm of men toward the top of the load, and they frantically began to remove the jumbled stack of planks. Al, the trapped foreman, was trying to control his moans as two crewmen tried to ease the pressure on his trapped leg. It seemed an interminably long time until his leg was finally freed, and he was carefully lowered to the ground where he was rushed to the nearest hospital. His leg and foot required extensive surgery and three steel pins.

Unloading the boxcars full of aggregates could be its own special purgatory in the summer. The sliding boxcar doors could not be opened until about half of the grain was unloaded, so the unfortunate worker with the scoop shovel had to work in almost unbearable heat.

Sometimes two men would be assigned to unload the boxcar, but more often only one. The sweltering heat would open the sweat pores only to have them caked with aggregate dust. Carloads of fertilizer were even worse because of their powerful acrid stench. These were days to be endured and then go back to mixing cattle feed and handling hundred-pound sacks.

The pickup sitting beside the road for sale was a 1964 Chevrolet Fleetside. Michael liked the way it looked, and the price was right so he decided to buy it to use for work. He had the cash, so at his first opportunity, he stopped in and bought it. The rear tires were worn out, so he saved up enough money to replace them with a pair of very expensive Michelin super grip tires. He drove the truck a few months then decided to invest in a body repair and new paint job. The call was made to Milford Eberly from the Glendale church. Milford said he would do the job for him, but it would be a while before he could get to it. Michael took the truck to Milford's shop then let the insurance lapse until it was finished.

One month passed, then two. There was no progress on the body job. A couple more months went by with no progress, so finally Michael began to pressure Milford to get it done. Once, he drove over to his shop to talk to him about it. Milford was not there, but one of the new Michelin tires was missing from the truck, and the axel was resting on a concrete block. Michael assumed it had lost air pressure, and they had removed it for repair. He could not have been more wrong! Months later when the truck was finally finished, he was shocked to discover that at least half of the tread was worn off the formerly missing tire. Milford had been "borrowing" it for his truck the whole time. Michael was shocked and very disappointed about it, but since he was still rather insecure, it was not in him to approach and adult about something like this. He paid the bill and drove away in silence.

# THE REAL FARM

One evening when the Raptors were at Uncle Gary's for a wiener roast, Carl confided in Uncle Gary that he was thinking about getting back into farming.

"Well, the Bonners are retiring and planning to sell their farm and all the assets together," Gary remarked. "The place needs some improvements and upgrades, but that would be a great way to jump right into farming."

Charlotte was not very excited about making the move from the little farm they now had all fixed up. It was the nicest home they had ever owned. But she was willing to check out the Bonner farm with Carl for his sake. She knew he had been unsatisfied at the window and door company and had always loved farming despite his lack of aptitude.

The next week, they made the twenty-five-mile drive to the Bonner farm to check it out. They were pleasantly surprised by what they saw.

The farm was two hundred and forty acres with about two-thirds of it was good tillable farm ground. The sixty-thousand-dollar price included the house, barn, silo, and a large machinery shed, as well as a herd of milk cows, heifers, two tractors, and a full line of machinery.

The equipment was older but in working condition, since the Bonners had been using it for their livelihood. It was a great buy, but sixty thousand dollars was still a lot of money, and they would need to borrow much of it. Carl began looking for financing. The idea of being his own boss and working at home was very appealing to him.

He also had big boys still living at home who could help with the farm work.

The next couple months were a yoyo of raised and dashed hopes as he applied to banks for financing and they declined the loans. Finally, when it became clear that banks were not interested in lending him the money, they began to lose hope.

But the many farmers in the Clayton church knew how to borrow money for farming. They recommended that he apply to a lending organization called FHA, so Carl went through their complicated loan application process, then they waited for the verdict. The wait seemed endless. And then suddenly it was over! Carl and Charlotte were summoned to a closing meeting with the Bonners, and the farm was theirs.

It being a dairy farm, the twice daily milking chores began almost immediately. They helped Mr. Bonner a couple times to learn the procedure, then they were on their own. Spring planting was just around the corner, so Carl needed to give the farm his fulltime attention. Their small farm sold fairly quickly, and their address was now Shaleville, a small town of around three hundred people. Their new nearest town had a bank, a grocery store, a hardware store, and a fairly large John Deere dealership. But it was much smaller than Smithville, with only a fraction of the bigger town's stores and businesses.

It was not necessary for the boys to change schools. The Clayton church had a well-established parochial school where Johnnie and Eli would attend. After some discussion, Michael and his parents agreed that he would finish his high school education through an accredited correspondence school program. It turned out to be a very good decision. He enjoyed the self-study courses, and while he was not able to enjoy a formal graduation like his older brothers, his education was thorough, and his diploma was valid. The high school diplomas from the Mennonite parochial schools, while highly prized by the students, were as worthless as the paper they were printed on. Those graduates who wanted a valid high school diploma needed to study to get a general education diploma, known as a GED. Most Mennonite parochial school graduates didn't bother but went straight into the job market—nearly all of them as farmers or tradesmen apprentices.

The Clayton school was a very big part of the church children's lives. They had a reasonably good educational program and usually managed to find people willing to teach who took the job seriously, although none of them had actual academic teaching credentials.

Most of the children attending the school were normal, energetic kids who loved studying and playing with their peers. The teachers tried to keep a lid on how rowdy they got as well as regulate the types of games they played. Games like "cops and robbers" were deemed inappropriate for a denomination who emphasized so strongly their claim to be nonresistant. Some of the boys came up with some rather creative workarounds such as relabeling the game 'anabaptists and persecutors.' One teacher, however, joined the children on the roof of the school for games and activities. The children thought it was great! The parents thought it was not great!

The Clayton church had long been plagued with sex scandals. Each generation had their moral blowouts, and while there was not necessarily any direct generational connection, the moral failures seemed to continue. The current generation was struggling with several cases of it. Some of the children seemed to see it as a pleasure game.

The problem had mostly been dealt with by the time the Raptors joined the church and school, but there were still occasional failings among the children and the adults. This was a dynamic the Raptors had never been exposed to. Except for Uncle Rusty who was the generally acknowledged epitome of immorality, they had never known this dynamic in their church lives. The incidents were strictly dealt with as they occurred, and successful coverups were few and unsubstantiated.

But the gossip flowed freely, and there seemed to be no effort made to stem the tide. While whole sermons were devoted to how members must dress and wear their hair and places they must not attend, little was said about the vicious rumors and gossip-mongering that circulated through the congregation. Michael would see this pattern in nearly every conservative Mennonite congregation he would associate with in his lifetime. It had begun with some of his earliest memories as a preschool child. Every month the church ladies had what they called a "sisters' sewing circle," where they would get together in the church basement and make blankets and quilts for the needy people. Their work was beautiful, and the cause was directly in line with Christian living. There was only one fly in the proverbial ointment—the words that were often spoken on those occasions.

Michael remembered how many times, as small boys, he and Dode and sometimes another little boy or two would be playing on the floor of the church basement with their toys, and he would hear the busy ladies sitting around the quilt in progress start hashing someone in their church. The person being criticized was never present and never approached later about the subject of their alleged shortcoming.

One quilting day, Dode and his mom did not show up, and even she, the preacher's wife, had her perceived shortcomings thoroughly hashed. This was hurtful to Michael because of all the women in church, next to Grandma Raptor, Dode's mom was the kindest to him. To hear her hashed by the women of the church was so unsettling he felt like jumping up and defending her! Then at the Sunday morning service, he noticed the same ladies who had said such mean things about her were as nice and friendly as could be! But some of the things that were said of her that day at the sewing would remain in Michael's memory verbatim for the rest of his life.

Gossip and slander would be some of the strongest criteria he would struggle with in his decision whether to remain a Mennonite.

One of the few things Michael looked forward to each winter at the Clayton church was their winter week of Bible school. It was held over the Christmas holiday and the Clayton church fathers would invite preachers from other areas to come and teach. These preachers would bring their families and other young people from their churches, which made the week infinitely more interesting to the Clayton young folks.

The first year the Raptor boys attended, Corey had enthusiastically described the Indiana preacher's two good-looking daughters,

Elaine and Mindy, to Michael. He said that they were both a lot of fun, but Elaine, the younger girl was better looking. He claimed he had tried to start a relationship with Elaine, but she was not as open as Mindy, so he ended up having a great time with Mindy. "You won't be able to help yourself from falling for those girls!" he predicted emphatically. Michael was rather skeptical. He knew Corey was a lady's man who got enthused about some girls whom he didn't think were all that great.

Michael was with Corey when he first saw the preacher's daughters, and he was mightily impressed with the raven-haired Elaine. She was one of the best-looking girls he had ever seen. Although Sherri had left a permanent imprint on his heart, he had not seen or heard from her in months, and he knew she had interest in another guy from North Dakota. They had no commitment of exclusivity, and both were free to explore other relationships. And this looked like a relationship worth pursuing! Over the course of the week, they were drawn to each other.

The week was always packed with social events, most of them centered around winter sports. Sledding and skating parties were numerous after Bible school dismissed in the early afternoons, and sometimes there were indoor social events in the evenings. Michael could tell that Elaine was attracted to him as well, but she seemed to have inhibitions toward furthering a relationship. He would learn in years to come that she was afflicted by an uber-religious nature which inhibited her ability to enjoy things that were not overtly religious in nature. She was more comfortable with another person between her and the object of her interest. Once when they ended up sitting beside each other in the backseat of a car, she got out and let someone get in between her and Michael. Corey had witnessed this, and later told Michael, "Boy, she sure doesn't want you. But sometimes she acts like she does! She's kind of hard to figure out."

In the weeks following, weeks after all the visitors had gone home from the Bible School, Elaine faded from Michael's mind. There were other fun girls who were a lot more ready to reciprocate than she had been, and life went on. But Elaine had not forgotten him. Some months later, she convinced her younger brother Wayne, who had also been at the Bible school, to call Michael and invite him to come and visit. The call confused Michael. He had liked Wayne, but he was several years younger than him and had mostly hung out with the younger guys like Johnny. He wondered if Elaine had put him up to the call but couldn't imagine what reason he could give for going down to visit them when she had acted so standoffish! He didn't pursue the invitation, but Elaine continued to lurk faintly at the back of his mind.

# "Driving Like a Fool?"

One afternoon, Michael was headed home after work in the mustang. He never got tired of driving the sporty little car. It hugged the road and like his live mustang Pal from the reservation, the sporty little car was always ready to leap forward at his slightest command. There was still a light rain falling from the heavy rainstorm that had just passed, and the road was wet and sloppy. He was cruising at a normal rate of speed when he topped a rise which fell away to a creek below. There was a narrow bridge with high steel frameworks on each side over the creek which would allow two cars to pass it they were careful. Unfortunately, there was a car sitting on the bridge, leaving only a narrow gap for a car to pass.

With only seconds separating them, Michael had to brake hard to try to get stopped in time. The light mustang went into a skid on the wet pavement, and Michael let off the brakes to try to get it straightened out. He was on the bridge now and trying to steer through the narrow gap between the parked car and the steel side rails of the bridge. The car struck the steel support which threw it semi-airborne down the opposite ditch into the trees. Michael was still wearing his hard hat from work that day, and it absorbed what would have been serious impacts from the roof and windshield. He climbed out of the mangled Mustang in time to see the stalled car being pushed off the bridge to the side of the road. He was a bit dazed from the drama and the impact, but also surprised that he was unhurt.

The car was off the bridge and out of the way before the police arrived. A passing motorist offered to call for help and agreed to call Michael's home as well as the police. A county deputy arrived and made out the accident report. With the car off the bridge where its occupants assured the officer it had been all along, there was no obvious reason for the accident. The officer issued Michael a citation for driving "too fast for conditions." He obviously believed the occupants of the stalled car over Michael's story that it had been partially blocking the bridge.

Finally, Michael saw the family car pull up to the scene with Charlotte at the wheel. In his shaken state, she was a welcome sight. She was looking at the mangled Mustang wrapped around the tree when Michael climbed in the car. He assumed that his mother would be as relieved as he was that he had escaped unharmed. As soon as he had closed the door behind him, she wheeled on him with fire in her eyes. "*Driving like a fool!*" she snarled.

Michael was speechless! His wellbeing had not even entered his mother's mind! "No," he replied, "that car was on the bridge when I came over the rise." He could see that she had already decided that it had been his fault, so they drove home in icy silence. In the following days, he struggled with the fact that his mother had totally not seemed to care about whether he was hurt or not. He chided himself for caring when he knew she didn't, but it was hard to bury the need of a child to be cared for.

The Mustang was towed to the body shop in nearby Shaleville. Fortunately, it was fully insured, and when the body shop owner said it was totaled, he told him he wanted it repaired anyway. It would be months until it was repaired, and Michael needed wheels to get to work. He had a few hundred dollars saved, so he prevailed on Randy to take him car shopping. After visiting a few towns and dealerships, he found what he had been looking for. The car was a coppery-brown Buick. There was nothing cool about the car; it was a four-door sedan with a rather uncommon four-speed automatic transmission. But it was affordable and ran well, so he forked over four hundred dollars and drove it home. He only planned to drive it until the mustang was repaired then sell it again.

As the Mustang repairs progressed, Michael had a strong desire to paint it burnt orange like a gorgeous sports car he had once seen. Like most sporty models of the day, the Mustang boasted a black vinyl roof, which he thought would set off the burnt orange color nicely. But there was one problem—the Clayton church rule book. While the long list of rules didn't specifically forbid burnt orange cars, that plan was very much not in sync with the way things were done there. Randy recommended that he check with their uncle, Bishop Neil. Michael thought that might be a good idea, so one evening, he called Bishop Neil. He could tell over the phone that his bishop/uncle was caught rather off guard by the request, but he told Michael he did not think that would be a problem and thanked him for checking about it. Michael was very enthused about how the newly painted car would look and eager to get it back from the body shop.

Then a few evenings later, his hopes were dashed. The telephone rang after supper, and Charlotte told Michael the call was for him. It was Bishop Neil. He said that they had discussed the idea of having the car painted burnt orange, and some of the other ministers were very opposed to the idea, so he was supporting them and forbade Michael to go ahead with that color. Michael was disappointed and frustrated! What difference did it make to the preachers what color his car was? The entire basis of the Mennonite religion was based on the salvation of fallen man through the redeeming sacrifice of God's son, Jesus. When that sacrifice was finished, the church leaders of that day gathered together to determine how much legalism could still be applied to genuine Christin living. They came up with four rules which were recorded in Acts 15 verses 28 to 29. These rules were given as the necessary rules.

But there has always been something in mankind that wants to contribute to his own salvation, and that need is the most easily filled by church rules and bylaws. When that path is followed unchecked, painful and destructive consequences often follow in the form of infighting, self-righteousness, judgmental condemnation, legalism, and many others. In the pursuit of all these church governmental politics, leading lost souls to redemption is a nebulous ideal. The justifying concept for them is the two verses in the Bible that speak of Gentiles being impressed with your good works and crediting God as the source.

What frustrated Michael and many of his peers was that the four original rules for the church had swelled into pages of rules in the Mennonite and other churches. Michael could not imagine any Gentile looking at a burnt orange Mustang and sadly shaking their head with some comment like, "God cannot possibly be honored by a burnt orange Mustang!"

After work the next day, he stopped in at the body shop to tell the owner that he was not allowed to change the color to burnt orange and they would just repaint it the original pale green. The body man suggested that they paint the area between the taillights flat black, so Michael agreed, and when it was finished, the car looked great!

# EIGHTEEN

One evening before bedtime, Michael was deeply engrossed in a book when the telephone rang. Charlotte answered, and he could tell it was Carl Jr. calling home. His mother visited with him for a while then called Michael to the phone.

"How's it going?" he heard his brother asked in his deep rumble.

"Oh, about like usual," Michael responded. "Nothing really new or exciting."

"I wondered if you would like to come out here for a while," Carl Jr. asked. "I can get you a job where I work, and Grandpa and Grandma said you could live with them."

Michael felt a stir of excitement. The thought had never occurred to him. As much as he would like to leave home, he had nowhere to go. He had been struggling to break the iron control his parents had tried to maintain over his life. The US congress had recently passed the twenty-sixth amendment lowering the legal age of adulthood from twenty-one to eighteen. On June 22, 1971, their state had ratified the amendment, but even the magical age of eighteen seemed a long, two-year wait for Michael.

When he had finally turned eighteen, he began trying to make decisions for himself. His mother had always been quick to punish him by not allowing him to attend social functions with his friends and young people. One morning as he was perusing the calendar on the dining room wall, he noticed that one of his friends from the Glendale youth group was planning to get married the following month. "Amanda's wedding is next month," he remarked out loud.

"I don't know if you will be going to that," Charlotte had declared rather unpleasantly.

Michael felt a wave of resentment wash over him. "I don't know either," he said pointedly. "I will have to decide that!"

Charlotte made no reply as she busied herself at the kitchen sink. These confrontations were becoming more frequent, with neither giving in. Michael often wondered why they even wanted him around home. All he could figure out was that it was their need to control him.

Now he finally had an opportunity to leave, and he contemplated the ramifications eagerly! "I would be very interested!" he replied. "I would need to give my boss a week or two notice, then I could head that way!"

"Okay," Carl Jr. responded, "I will make arrangements on this end and we will see you in a couple weeks."

The next two weeks flew by as Michael gave notice to his boss and packed to head east. He left in the predawn darkness and as the sporty green Mustang hummed over the highway, he felt a first ever thrill of freedom. He didn't know what lay ahead of him, but he was sure there would be new adventures and the wonderful freedom to make his own decisions and live his own life without all the criticism and deprecation. Having visited Grandpa Raptors several times, he had a fair idea of the beauty of their hills and mountains and their narrow, twisting country roads.

Grandpa, Grandma, and Aunt Leona welcomed him with open arms. He was given a bedroom up on the third floor of their house, which he found cozy and gave him a remarkable view out over the neighborhood. As the weeks passed, he was continually surprised and honored by the respect they all showed him. Aunt Leona was in a dating relationship and, as usual, was facing the need to choose between interested suitors. When he got to know them better, Michael thought they were both great guys. Aunt Leona was older than Carl Jr., but Michael came to love and respect her as the big sister he had never had. She very tactfully gave him guidance in some of his remaining areas of cultural shortcomings.

The job on the construction crew was interesting as well as a bit challenging physically. The owner ran several crews who did everything from concrete work and masonry, to framing and finished carpentry. Carl Jr. had worked his way up to job foreman, and Michael often found himself on his crew. The most brutal work they did was concrete block laying. Michael, who had no block-laying experience, always ended up being the "mud-boy" a very undesirable position to fill. He was always impressed by his big brother's building skills, but Carl Jr. assured him that before they had taught him how to lay block and brick, he had done his time as mud-boy as well.

Being mud-boy consisted of keeping the block layers supplied with fresh blocks to lay and fresh mortar to lay them with. The layers enjoyed yelling at the sweating mud-boy if they ran short of blocks up on their scaffold or if they ran out of mortar or if the mortar was not the precise, preferred consistency, or just for the fun of persecuting the young victim! Michael worked hard to please them, and their rare compliments gave him an unreasonable thrill of pride. He usually enjoyed being on Carl Jr.'s crew and often thought that his big brother was less bossy as his official boss than he had been at home in their growing up years. They usually rode to the job together in Carl Jr.'s new international half-ton pickup truck. Michael thought the truck was kind of a tin can for a new pickup, but Carl Jr. rammed the poor swaying beast through the Reading Pa rush hour traffic like Ben Hur in his chariot race. The guys on the crew called the truck a "corn binder," and Carl Jr. used the same term for the fire-engine-red vehicle.

The hourly pay rate was not great for flunkies like Michael, but they were always able to put in overtime hours for extra pay which usually earned them a decent paycheck. Sometimes on days when they poured concrete, they had to stay late into the night to work the concrete as it dried. One day, they poured the basement floor in a new house in a remote location up in the hills where there were no neighbors. The concrete was drying so slowly that Carl Jr. told the rest of the crew they could go home, and he and Michael would come back after supper to finish working it smooth. He took Michael along home for supper, and afterward he invited Linda along with them to hang out at the job until he finished up.

When they arrived back at the job, he gave Michael some unskilled projects to complete while he operated the power troweler over the newly poured basement floor. Linda strolled around the project looking at the landscape and stacks of building materials. The house was framed, and the roof was on, but they had not yet begun to finish the inside.

The concrete was setting up extra slowly and Carl Jr. continued to work it as it became full dark. The electricians had not yet begun to install the lighting, so the construction crew had strung temporary work lights in the basement to work on the concrete project. There was some light filtering up the stairway, and Linda decided to sit at the top of the stairway to wait for Carl Jr. to finish the job. Michael had finished his assignments and was fast getting bored. He decided to have a little fun at his new sister-in-law's expense.

Unseen by her, he crept to the far end of the house and climbed up into the trusses onto the plywood that had been nailed the length of the house. He began to crawl slowly toward the other end where Linda sat at the top of the stairs, watching her husband work the concrete with the noisy power troweler. As he crawled, he made weird scratching noises and soon was rewarded by seeing his sister-in-law casting nervous glances to the catwalk above her. He would give her a few moments to calm her fears then crawl a bit closer with the accompanying sound effects. He could see her nervousness increasing and felt a twinge of shame for pranking such a nice, gentle lady, but the opportunity was too good to pass up, so he continued his terrorizing progress.

Eventually, Michael was directly over Linda's head, and he could see that she was really getting anxious. There had been reports lately of several heinous murders in the area which had folks a bit spooked. Linda had no place to go because the only light was in the basement where her husband was focused on the setting concrete. Michael decided to up the ante with a few weird hissing sighs to accompany the scratching and creaking noises. Linda called his name a few times, but the last she had seen him, he had been out behind the house, and she had not seen him come in. Finally, in desperation, she called out to Carl Jr. In spite of her fear, her voice was still cultured and ladylike. The irony of her call cracked Michael's composure, and he howled with laughter! Linda graciously forgave him, but he could tell that his big brother was rather irritated by the stunt when they told him about it later.

Pranks on the job were normal occurrences, however. One of the favorites was to catch someone using the portable wooden outhouse. The crew would watch for one of the flunkies to enter the outhouse and shut the door, then a couple of the workers would sneak up and screw the door shut so he couldn't get out. If it was a hot day, they might leave him in there to cook for a while, but the favorite prank was for one man to stand on each side and flop the little structure from side to side with the hapless victim inside flopping helplessly from one wall to the other, trying not to pick up a splinter in his posterior!

They were working on a new house in the trees one day, where the driveway wound through thick trees and underbrush. It was not possible to see approaching vehicles until they had rounded the last bend which was very close to the house. The crew had caught Michael in the outhouse and were just beginning to give him a vigorous rocking when suddenly it stopped, and the door was quickly opened for him. He saw his two tormenters slinking back to the house then realized what had happened. They had just started the rocking when the boss's truck had appeared at the curve and he had caught them in the act. After that, they were much more cautious with that prank.

But they were always alert for more opportunities. One hot summer day, they were shingling the roof of a beautiful new home which boasted a fireplace in the basement and another on the main floor. The two chimneys rose side by side at the end of the house above the roof. After lunch break, Michael was the first one back up the ladder onto the roof, and while he waited for the others, what at the time seemed like a great idea occurred to him. He would crawl down into one of the chimney flues and hang by his fingers, then when the others got up on the roof, he would pop up and shout at them.

He was about to discover several fatal flaws in the plan. He was able to get a little more than halfway down when he realized that the flues were not large enough to accommodate his entire body. When he decided to abort the plan, he discovered that he was unable to pull himself back out. He was stuck in the flue from the main floor fireplace with his head hanging over the flue from the basement fireplace.

Michael was not claustrophobic, but he had to control the urge to panic in his situation. When a couple more workers appeared on the roof, he called for help. They took their time walking over and assessing his situation then began to chuckle at his explanation of why he was in this situation. They were still chuckling as they disappeared back down the ladder to tell the rest of the crew, leaving Michael stuck in the chimney. He began to yell for help, but help was not forthcoming. He heard noises coming up the basement chimney, then to his horror, smoke began rising through that flue! "We will smoke you out!" someone yelled up from below. The workers howled with laughter as Michael swung his head from side to side to avoid the smoke. Finally, the laughter died down, and two of the men grabbed him by the shoulders and hoisted him out of the chimney flue. He had not inhaled enough smoke to do any damage, but it was some time before he got rid of the smoke stench. He rather liked the way the guys kidded around and had fun on the job, but he wished they would pick on each other a bit more often rather than the "flunky."

Pennsylvania had a rich culture which was highlighted by the large number of Amish in this area. Michael, always a horse lover, was fascinated by how the Amish culture centered around horses. There were the tall and lean, high-stepping horses pulling the back buggies down the road, and then there were the huge, heavily muscled draft horses with enormous hooves pulling the wagons and farm equipment. The most fascinating of all though were the gangly little foals cavorting around the pastures each spring on their knobby knees and stick-thin legs.

The Amish men were known for their homemade clothes and straw hats. The men were not allowed to shave their beards once they joined the church and got married. The women wore long, shapeless, dark-colored dresses which they made themselves, and they were not allowed to cut or trim their hair. The little girls' hair was braided until they got into their teens at which time the hair was coiled into a "bun" and pinned on top of their heads under a large white veiling-shaped like an inverted basket with strings dangling or tied under the chin.

Most of the Amish lived on farms with huge barns and very large houses. Often, there would be a smaller house on the farm where grandma and grandpa would live until they passed away, then it would be used again for the next retired couple. As time went on there was not enough land available for oncoming generations to farm, so they began to branch out into construction businesses, repair shops, food and bakery stores, and other enterprises. Amish craftsmen were often preferred for the quality and durability of their workmanship.

Michael never tired of the beautiful, mountainous scenery in this state. One cool, damp morning, he and Carl Jr. had been dispatched to a home up in the hills for some roof repairs on a garage. They worked as the sun gradually rose and warmed things up, then about midmorning they stopped for a break. Carl Jr. disappeared around behind the garage to find a convenient tree to irrigate. "Come here for a minute," he said when he returned, "I want to show you something."

Michael followed him into the garage and stared in fascination at the gorgeous orange Datsun 240z in the right bay. He thought he had never seen a car so cool or so beautiful. "I thought you would like it," Carl Jr. said with a grin. "It's a real beauty!" The car was in like-new condition with a black leather interior that fairly begged someone to climb in and fire it up! Michael would have been happy to oblige, but fortunately there was on key in the ignition. In years to come, he would own many sporty muscle cars including a high-performance Dodge Charger and a Corvette Stingray, but he never owned one more impressive than the sporty little orange Datsun.

Carl Jr. got along well with most of the men in the company, but he hit it off extra with a smaller man named Matt. Matt was a hardworking, fun-loving guy who seemed to have a smile on his face all the time. Everyone seemed to like him a lot, and he was full of jokes and funny stories to share as they worked. One day, Michael was assigned to work with him at a job about an hour's drive from the shop. They talked about all kinds of subjects in the course of the day, but Michael was shocked when Matt asked him about an incident of abuse from his childhood. Michael was dumbfounded and stared at Matt, not knowing what to say. It was one of those incidents that he had not even discussed with his brothers. He wasn't trying to hide or deny them, but there were just some things so ugly he didn't know how to talk about!

"Sorry," Matt said at length. "I wasn't trying to bring up something you don't want to talk about. Your brother just shared with me how things kinda went in your home, and it must have been pretty tough!"

"Yeah," Michael mumbled, "it was pretty messed up."

Michael thought a lot about their past in the following days. *Why could he and his brothers not talk about what had gone on? It didn't need to be continually hashed, but the covering up and pretending all was well was not even honest!* He had tried to talk to his mother about it, but she had literally mocked and mimicked him, and all but told him he was making it up! He knew that different people handled things different ways. Randy was always one to minimize and pass off the nasty things in life with "it wasn't really all that bad." Randy, however, had rarely gotten the really rough treatment. The uncontrolled beatings with their father's face twisted, teeth clenched, and eyes blazing cold fury were mostly visited on Michael and Carl Jr. But while it was easy to talk to Randy about most things, that subject was untouchable unless he wanted to hear again that he was bringing it on himself because he was such a bad kid. So he learned to bottle it up inside as his own anger and resentment had continued to build. He knew his father was a basically good man with a lot of abilities and integrity, but this one weakness, coupled with his inability to acknowledge and apologize for his brutality, had totally destroyed any chance at a genuine father and son relationship with his older sons.

But while Michael was haunted by the past, he had learned to move on and live life in the present, and life had been continually improving the last few years. Lately, he had been contemplating getting into the dating scene. He had always had interests and relationships with girls but had never felt free to officially begin a dating relationship. Aunt Leona had been giving him some counsel and pointers and had even offered to double date with him if it would make him more comfortable. She was dating a super nice guy named Bill who had a female cousin, who Michael thought was nice, so they arranged a double date to a concert.

The concert was good, and the evening was enjoyable, but Michael was very ill at ease with the young lady. She seemed poised and reasonably comfortable, but Michael felt like he was blowing the relationship before it ever got started. It was his first and only date in Pennsylvania, but he later felt like it had been a good learning experience.

Grandma and Grandpa Raptor continued to shower him with love and kindness. He agreed with Randy who had always maintained that they were as close to perfect as grandparents can get. There was really nothing that he disliked about this state or living with them, but as the summer gave way to fall, he very much began missing his friends back home. He had had some contact with Johnny who was becoming a young man in his own right and Michael missed him too. But he especially missed Nate and his Birchwood buddies, and the good times they had had together. One day, Nate called him to tell him that he had moved to Southern Indiana and was working for a carpenter crew there. He told Michael he would like him to move down there too, but Michael had been thinking more about going back to Ohio.

When Michael finally made the decision to move back to Ohio, it was hard for Grandpa's and Carl Jr. to understand, but they were supportive and courteous about it. When the day came, he packed the green mustang and headed west. He would often wonder if he had made the right decision.

# BELL-BOTTOM TROUSERS

Back in Ohio, he hired on at the feed mill again and paid his room and board at home by remodeling the upstairs of the old farmhouse. He tried to keep his interactions with his parents as amicable as possible, but they made it obvious that they did not like him hanging out with his Birchwood buddies. To their credit, they were always polite and hospitable to them on the relatively few occasions when Michael brought them home, but especially Charlotte made it plain that she would rather see him hang out with his more conservative Clayton friends and cousins.

But things up at Birchwood just kept getting better! They cruised around town, found places to eat, and hang out and talked, joked, and laughed a lot. Nate's cousins were more knowledgeable in hanging out and having fun, and their parents gave them no grief about it. All the boys had been raised with strict moral standards, and their fun, while not acceptable to the rigidly conservative parents concerned about maintaining appearances, was not immoral. They neither swore, drank, stole, nor indulged in any type of immorality. Many times, they would just hang out in one of their homes and talk or play guitar.

One weekend, Michael rode up to Birchwood with Randy who was going to spend the weekend with Maria and her family. They took Randy's Chevy and he instructed Michael to just drop him off and he could use the car for the weekend. The car was nothing special, and it had one bad habit—the brakes. It had a standard shift transmission, and the brakes worked fine for the first few minutes, but if you held them longer, they would lose pressure and disengage.

Little idiosyncrasies like this in cars were not unusual. The driver just had to remember them and work around them.

After dropping Randy off, Michael headed for Nate's house to pick him up. Then they picked up his cousins and headed for town.

In the course of the evening, Nate's older cousin Wilbur ended up behind the wheel as they cruised around town. Michael had warned him about the car's bad brakes, but he didn't seem to be concerned. Driving around town, they spotted a police car, and somehow Wilbur thought it would be entertaining to follow him around town. They followed him for ten or fifteen minutes, turning every time he turned. Finally, the officer got tired of the game and wheeled into a parking lot and made a fast circle bringing him up behind the Chevy. Some of the guys were getting rather nervous as the officer began to follow them around town, matching turn for turn. But Wilbur just laughed and said they had done nothing illegal and had nothing to worry about.

His confidence was soon put to the test when the trooper lit them up with his red strobes. Wilbur pulled to the side on a slight incline and rolled down his window. The officer pulled his car up close behind and got out to approach the Chevy. Wilbur and his brother got a bit sassy with him and his temper began to flare. They had been arguing for a few minutes when the old Chevy decided to join the fun. The brakes bled off, and she rolled back into the grille of the police cruiser with a satisfying thud! They all piled out to examine the damage with the officer, then a new line of argument began between the officer who was threatening to write Wilbur up for a vehicle defect and Wilbur, who was telling him that he had parked too close behind him and had it coming!

Michael was torn between the adrenaline high from what they had been doing, and the nagging knowledge that Randy was going to nail his hide to the wall for this! Amazingly, there was no discernable damage to the police cruiser and very little to the Chevy. Wilbur got off with a warning which seemed to bother him not at all!

One of the guys Michael liked a lot was a good-natured guy named Lane. Lane seemed to see the humor in everything, and he had the ability to make Michael laugh just by looking at him with his goofy grin. Lane was not as concerned about the latest fashionable clothes as some of the other guys, although his parents were very tolerant of most of his behavior. Nate was a snappy dresser, and Michael often felt a bit dowdy when hanging out with him. Flared and bell-bottom trousers were all the rage, and that was what Nate wore. Michael's mother hounded him mercilessly when he attempted to wear them. Then fashion upped the ante another notch by introducing flares with cuffs. Michael simply went to the store and bought himself a pair and began wearing them. The torch of criticism at home became an instant flamethrower! He knew there was no way he could buy another pair without having the house go up in flames, so he contented himself with that one pair which he knew he wore too often.

One day, he heard one of his buddies comment to another about how often he wore those same trousers. Michael was hurt by the criticism, but he knew there was no way these guys would ever understand the intense pressures he lived with at home. He had never really considered moving out and getting his own apartment. The optics of that would have started world war three! What would the Clayton people think of one of the kids from the wonderful Raptor family doing such a thing? He would have most likely lost his church membership over such a stunt! One of his older cousins from a similar family had actually bought a small travel trailer and moved into the woods where he worked. That became a subject spoken of only behind hands shielding gossiping mouths. The best course was to move out of state.

When Nate mentioned to Michael that their church was getting ready for summer Bible school, Michael didn't take much notice. But when he saw the carload of girls who had come from Indiana to teach, his interest sharpened immensely! Sherri's family had moved to another state, which was a huge relief to his mother, and their relationship had evaporated more than dissolved. There had been other cute girls who had attracted him, but none with the magnetism of Sherri Bannon!

There were several cuties in the group, but his interest was especially caught by one named Megan. She was outgoing as well as attractive, and when some of his buddies began to ask the girls out, he worked up the courage to ask her. She readily agreed, and they were soon spending every spare minute together. There was no awkwardness between them as there had been on his first date, and Michael had finally figured out that these cute girls were not just kissing him for his benefit! But there was a firm line in the relationships, and they never became sexual in nature. Neither of them followed up the relationship when she returned home, however, so it too evaporated when she left. Michael would always think of her as a very fine young lady who had spent some quality time together with him for one memorable summer week!

# THE HAREM HAULER

Nate was getting restless to leave again. He tried to talk Michael into going to Southern Indiana with him, but Michael was reluctant. Getting to know a whole new set of people was not something that appealed to him, so Nate and his cousin moved down without him. Life for Michael became such a drag that he eventually moved down and joined them. Nate helped him get a job with a Mennonite construction crew who treated him well. The company was owned by an older man, and his grown sons helped him manage it and run the crews.

Michael found the work familiar and reasonably enjoyable. They boarded with a young fellow named Stan, who was about their age. His parents were gone for the winter, so they had the place to themselves. They got along well with Stan, and he liked to party as well as they did. Stan had friends and relatives in the nearby Amish community who came and partied with them. They played a lot of music and talked and laughed a lot. Michael was amazed at how well the Amish fellows could play their guitars. All musical instruments are strictly and totally forbidden in the Amish faith, so the guys had to hide their guitars under the hay in the haymows and sneak them out to go party. It was the most enjoyable time of Michael's life to date. But it could not last forever, and several months later, Stan related the pronouncement of doom. His parents would be returning the following week. Nate and Michael spent much time discussing their immediate future. Nate had had his share of problems with his preacher father when he lived under his roof, and in Michael's perception, moving back home was tantamount to living in a war zone.

But although Stan had assured them that his parents were fine with them continuing to board there and that they would impose no rules on them. Neither of them could imagine such a scenario. They sat up late several nights discussing their options. Michael tried to talk Nate into going to Pennsylvania with him, but Nate was not interested. These late-night discussions continued each night with each succeeding night becoming more urgent. Finally, it was the last night before Stan's parents returned, and they sat up discussing the situation until well after midnight. The pressure was enormous, and a decision had to be made this night!

"Let's just go home," Nate said. "We can figure out what to do from there."

"That looks like our only option," Michael agreed, let's pack up and go!"

In total stealth, they carried all their belongings downstairs and packed them in their cars. When it was finished, they composed a note to their employer then slipped into Stan's room to say goodbye. Stan had a hard time coming fully awake, and his sleep-addled brain had difficulty absorbing what they were telling him. He could see no reason why things had to change. He had always gotten along great with his parents and couldn't grasp why these two buddies saw them as an obstacle! But he finally let it go and agreed to contact their boss in the morning with the note.

Dawn was only a couple hours away as the two buddies climbed into their sports cars and headed them north. Nate took the lead in his Nova SS, and before long, Michael noticed that he appeared to be showing the effects of sleep deprivation. It seemed to get worse as the dawn began streaking across the horizon, then finally Nate pulled his car over on the shoulder and came back to the Mustang. "I'm having trouble staying awake," he said, stating the obvious. "I can stay awake if I drive faster. If you want to keep up fine, otherwise I will see you back home." Michael had heard several remedies for staying awake at the wheel, but this was the first he had heard of this one!

"Okay," he said, "do what you need to do, and I will play it by ear."

Michael tried to keep up with the streaking blue Nova for a while, but finally his fear of cops made him ease off the accelerator. He really hoped his friend would make it home safely without a speeding ticket! He felt slightly uneasy about the speed of the Nova, but he had a lot of confidence in his buddy's driving.

Michael pulled in the drive to the farm as the sun was setting. There was no cozy feeling of homecoming. It was more akin to checking into a motel for a while. He had absolutely no idea what his future looked like, but things were happening in the family. Randy had gotten engaged to Maria from Birchwood, and they were planning for a wedding soon. Johnny was growing up and coming into his own as the "big boy" of the family with his older brothers coming and going. He always accused Michael of taking all the girls' attentions, but he was in fact getting his own share. He was also having his share of problems trying to become his own person. He was bound to a very strict curfew at midnight on evenings he was out with friends or church youth activities. His car was not especially cool, but it got him around, often with an assortment of young ladies needing a ride to social activities. Young Eli liked to refer to his car as his "harem hauler." Johnny, chief of the irritating verbal one-liners, eventually saw the need to take his irritating little brother down on the lawn and fill his mouth with fresh, green grass for his many verbal indiscretions.

One evening, Johnny was running a bit late getting home by curfew. He drove as fast as he dared but still arrived home a bit late. He tried to sneak up to his room, but the next morning, his parents began to berate him for missing curfew. Johnny had never been on the receiving end of the real rough physical treatment from his father, whose insane temper outbursts seemed to be lessening as he aged. But Charlotte had the ability to work her husband up into a white-hot rage when it suited her purposes against one of her sons.

The curfew exchange built into a domestic inferno when Carl demanded the keys to his son's car and Johnny refused. With the keys in his hand, Johnny dashed out into the lawn with his furious father hard on his heels. He knew he could easily outrun him, so he ran around the lawn just fast enough to stay ahead, with the keys flopping tantalizingly from his hand. Carl's face was twisted with fury, and he roared like a wounded grizzly bear. He ran with his arms stretched forward and his hands clenched into claws. But his recalcitrant son just kept running until he wore his father down and he returned to the house minus the keys. There was no further discussion of the incident.

Michael was amazed when Johnny related the story to him later. "I would never have even considered trying something like that with him!" he exclaimed. "Sooner or later, he would have gotten me, and I would have paid dearly for that stunt!"

Michael and Johnny's worlds turned more and more around cars. Cars got them away from home and took them to adventures. Cars carried their friends and special female friends. Some of their friends were getting powerful sports cars. Leighton had bought a powerful Mustang Mach 1, which he later traded in on a Corvette Stingray. He was always ready to take on any comers in an impromptu drag race. A family named Manning drove an Oldsmobile with a powerful engine for their family car. They had a son named Mark who was one of Johnny's best buddies. Mark didn't have his own car, but he loved taking the family Oldsmobile out and "clearing the carbon out of the engine."

There was a fairly long and flat stretch of County Road V running past the school. The south end of the flat stretch turned into a long curve, and at the north end was a short but steep blind hill. On the west side of the hill lived Charlotte's older married niece Janice Baker, and her family.

It would have been wiser for the occasional drag races to have begun on the hill and run south, but nobody wanted to line up for a drag race a hundred feet from Janice's front door! Janice didn't gossip any more or less than anyone else in church, but they knew word would get around.

One night, Johnny was cruising south on County Road V in the battered old farm pickup. There was no way he could know that Leighton and Mark had lined up, side by side at the school and were now streaking toward him at over ninety miles per hour. Johnny crested the hill in the pickup truck at exactly the same time as the two screaming cars, and his blood turned to ice! With no time for any of them to think, what happened next was mostly instinctive! Leighton floored the Corvette as Mark locked up his brakes. The Oldsmobile went into a skid and was sliding broadside on the asphalt toward Johnny who reflexively cranked his wheels toward the ditch! By some miracle, he had missed the Oldsmobile by mere inches.

Mark managed to get his car under control again, and a badly shaken young man headed for home. When Johnny's pickup plowed to a stop, he sat dazed for a few long minutes. He had cheated death by a hair's breadth and fast reflexes. He turned the truck around and headed for Mark's house. He arrived just as the black Oldsmobile was disappearing into the garage. Johnny had some choice and very emphatic words of rebuke to share with his young buddy, and he shared his thoughts in a manner that left no doubt as to his frame of mind!

Mark was still shaken by the incident, and he listened without protest then made a solemn vow that he would never race a car on the road again. To the best of Johnny's knowledge, he never did.

Unfortunately, the incident had been observed by the Bakers. Several days later, when Johnny walked into the farmhouse, he was greeted by a furious mother. "What happened on the school road the other night?" she asked angrily.

"A couple guys were racing, and I had to get out of their way," he replied. His mind whirled in confusion. *Why was she so angry? Did she think he had been racing?* "I wasn't racing," he clarified. "I was driving the truck."

"Well, why didn't you tell your parents about it?" she snarled. "How does that make us look? It's all over church and your parents don't even know about it!"

*Oh,* he thought as understanding began to dawn on him. *She is not angry about what happened or how nearly I got killed! She knows I wasn't racing, but she is embarrassed because it makes her look bad that I didn't confide in her. Don't they realize that any time we confide in them it comes back around to bite us in the butt?*

"If something like that ever happens again, you tell your parents immediately!" she demanded.

Wordlessly, Johnny turned around and walked out. *Uh-huh!* he thought, *that's really gonna happen!*

Over the next few years, there would be some tragic incidents connected to Baker's hill. One day, their young nephew was riding his bike and was struck by Mark's mother in the family car. He died from his injuries.

Sometime later, Janice's husband would be killed chasing after some boys who had been harassing his property. He was thrown from a pickup at a high rate of speed as they were chasing their vehicle and died from his injuries. Janice's father had died very young from a heart attack, and it seemed that her family had been visited with more than their share of heartbreak for decades afterward.

# RANDY'S LOVE NEST AND MICHAEL'S SHOWDOWN

Randy and Maria were planning their upcoming wedding. Randy had bought a very old tumbledown house just outside of Smithville with an equally tumbledown garage. It was situated in a sizeable tract of weedy and tree-shaded property and he paid $2,500 for it, then he borrowed another $6,000 to remodel it. It would have scared off most brides-to-be, but he had two things in his favor on that score. First, she was the daughter of a very good carpenter, so she understood how properties can be restored. Secondly, and perhaps the most important, she loved her man to distraction and would most likely have moved into a cow barn with him.

Michael and Johnny were a bit irritated by her near worship of their older brother. It seemed she could honestly not see one tiny flaw in him—an oversight which they certainly did not share! One day at a youth activity when she was there without Randy, Michael and Johnny took on the responsibility to set the record straight. Their attempted education ran off her like water off a duck's back.

"You guys are just mad at him about something that happened," she surmised. "He is not like that at all!"

While the two younger brothers' counsel may have been ill-advised, they actually weren't on a payback mission. They just wanted her to be a bit more realistic. Later in life, Michael would come to understand that there are two things in life that you never try to advise people about. One is love interests, whether courting or marriage. The other is their children. Nothing good ever comes from following your nose down those roads!

Randy leaned on Michael quite a bit to remodel the old house. His building experience with Uncle Don came in handy, and soon the house was gutted down to the very crooked framing. When the plaster, lath, and old lumber had been hauled away, they began the arduous labor of straightening walls and framing in the rooms the way they wanted them. There was electricity in the house but no running water or bathroom. Bathroom needs were dealt with out in the weeds. They were drinking a lot of soda, and this required many trips to the weeds. This was extra time-consuming when they were working upstairs.

Eventually they hit on a mileage-saving plan. They saved all the soda bottles and used them for urinals. When they were full, they would replace the caps then move on to the next bottle. Somehow, they never got around to throwing them out with the trash, and the bottles ended up in a row on the upstairs windowsill. One afternoon Randy was giving Maria the tour of their progress when her attention was drawn to the soda bottles lined up on the windowsill. She looked rather puzzled as she picked one up and unscrewed the cap. Michael was as embarrassed as Randy when they saw the realization hit her of what the bottles actually contained! They would laugh about it later, but at that moment, the situation was utterly devoid of humor!

Little by little, the shack took on a new life to become a cozy love nest for the newlyweds. The construction would go on for several years after their marriage, with the garage the last project on the agenda.

Randy was making decent money at his logging job, and he was seriously thinking about purchasing a new car. Except for wealthy big brother Carl Jr., purchasing new vehicles were never even seriously considered. Randy was looking at a new Chevy Vega, a rather nice-looking small car that was being offered at a surprisingly low price. One day, he made his final decision and drove the little white Vega off the dealer's lot. A few years later, he like many other new Vega owners, would come to regret this decision, but at the time it was a sweet little ride! He and Maria were planning a camping trip for their honeymoon, so Randy hatched up the idea of pulling a small one-wheel trailer behind it. The trailer carried a fair amount of cargo and required very little extra fuel and turned out to be a good idea in spite of predictions of doom from several people.

Things at home were not going well for Michael. There was a growing resentment on the part of his parents of his comings and goings without their permission. They were especially upset about his spending nearly every weekend with his Birchwood buddies. It helped that Nate's father was the bishop at Birchwood, but Michael's parents would really rather see him hang around with the Clayton guys.

One of his former boss' sons from southern Indiana was planning to get married to a northern Indiana gal, and Michael, Nate, and Lane made plans to attend the wedding. They would take Michael's Mustang and only be gone a few days. They left early one morning while it was still dark.

Lane was at the wheel, and Michael was half-dozing in the backseat when a large buck jumped from the weeds in the ditch directly in the path of the Mustang. They hit it with a sickening impact and slewed to a stop. The fender, grille, and hood were damaged, and the windshield was cracked. They limped back to the farm with it and transferred their bags to Nate's Nova and headed out again.

The weekend was very active and enjoyable, and it was great to see their friends from southern Indiana again. They made several new friends from the area, including a young fellow named Larry who was from a very conservative Mennonite home where he and his brother had been constantly fighting with their hot-tempered father. Larry finally left home and rented a room with a sympathetic young couple who had once attended their church. He had a very high-paying job at an RV manufacturing company and seemed to have plenty of money. He drove a customized Nova and drove it hard! There were a lot of young Mennonite and Amish guys in the area who had absolutely no interest in the rigid confines of the religious orders they had come out of. Some of their parents allowed them to live at home, and some kicked them out. There seemed to be plenty of places for them to go when they left home. Some rented their own apartments. These were the cool guys who were totally independent. Most of them had girlfriends. It seemed there was an abundant supply of attractive, fun-loving girls in this community, and Nate and Michael began to seriously discuss moving down to this area.

They were cruising some country roads one afternoon when Michael spotted an absolutely gorgeous Dodge Charger sitting by the road with a "For Sale" sign in the window. They stopped to look at it, and he knew at once that he would do everything in his power to buy this beauty. It was red with black stripes, chrome wheels, hideaway headlights, black vinyl roof, and a powerful 440 Magnum engine. The inside was leather, and it had every option available at the time of purchase. The owner was a well-off Amish kid who had decided to get married and join the Amish church where he had been raised. The car was in showroom condition, and his selling price was $3,500. Michael said he would buy it if he could get a loan.

He went to visit the banker who had loaned him the money for the Mustang who was surprisingly amenable to the idea and loaned him the money which he forwarded to the owner. Several weeks later, a friend from that area was able to bring the car up to him.

It would have been an enormous understatement to say that his parents did not approve of the purchase! They were shocked and very unhappy that he had managed to pull the purchase off on his own, not to mention their ever-present concern over how it might "make them look." But the Mustang was in the repair shop again, so Michael happily drove the mighty beast everywhere he went. The first time he drove it to church, one of the youth guys who drove a stodgy Chevy took him aside and forcefully warned him that he would "not get to heaven in that car!"

Michael stared at him for a long moment and said, "You know, I wasn't really planning to drive that car to heaven any more than you are planning to drive yours there!"

His accuser suddenly became noticeably nervous. "Pass it off," he said quickly, "just pass it off!"

Michael was not angry, but he was very irritated. This guy was a perfect example of what bugged him most about these church people. Many of them were quick to blab out their critical thoughts before their brain even got a chance to filter their mouths! Some of them seemed to take pride in the nasty and hurtful things they constantly said to and about others. Those tendencies were contagious, and there were too many times when he caught himself spouting unfiltered thoughts to his own embarrassment and chagrin.

Once, he had been visiting in someone's home when the wife informed her husband of some misdeeds that had been committed by another lady in church. The husband became incensed and snapped, "Well where does she come off acting like that?"

"You can't say anything about her that hasn't already been said," the wife replied.

*Wow!* Michael thought, *that covers a lot of territory! I'll bet God is real proud of these folks!*

Michael and Randy shared an upstairs bedroom in the old farm-house. Neither of them was home much, but they nearly always came home to sleep. The Mustang had been repaired and was back sitting in the driveway. Charlotte liked to drive it, but Michael had trans-ferred the insurance coverage from it to the Charger. One weekend, the Charger had a minor mechanical problem, so Michael decided to take the Mustang to Birchwood for the weekend. He got back late Sunday night and went straight to bed.

Randy was usually gone before Michael got up, and the next morning, Michael awoke to the sound of thundering feet stomping up the stairs and into his room. "Michael!" his father shouted. "You drove that Mustang up to Birchwood with *no insurance* on it!"

Michael looked up at the familiar scene of his furious father with his face twisted with rage. His mind went from zero to sixty miles an hour in a split second.

"Yes," he said calmly, in spite of the extreme tension. "I had a problem with the Charger, so I took the Mustang."

"Don't you *ever* drive a car without insurance!" Carl roared. "And there are a few more things that are gonna change around here. From now on, you *will* get our permission *every time* before you go up to Birchwood, and you *will* be home by curfew every night before work!"

Michael's brain was processing furiously. He was pretty sure he could hold his own now if it came to blows, and if he was attacked, he *would* fight back! He had vowed to never again stand and take a beating from this brute! He slowly drew back the blanket and stood to his feet, nose to nose with the furious man. He was cold and numb on the inside, but his voice was even and deadly calm as he responded.

"Okay," he said, "if that's how you feel, I will leave today, and I will not come back!"

He was bracing for the first blow when to his utter astonishment, the apoplectic man before him instantly lost his composure and crumbled! The fury in his eyes suddenly vanished, and confusion flickered there for a moment, then absolute defeat. His body which had been rigid with anger, literally slumped. "You...you can wait until after the wedding," Carl stammered. "You know you were planning to leave then, and so do we!"

Michael thought it over for a few seconds. He knew that their concern was not about losing him, but how it would make them look if he moved out before the wedding. "Okay," he replied, "I will wait if that is how you want it." Unsaid but mutually understood was the obvious conclusion that his list of new rules was a non-starter.

Michael almost felt sorry for the implosion of the once proud man before him. Almost! But more than that, for the first time in his life, he realized that his father was a bully! He knew his father had always been a God-fearing man, who was admired by many for his humor and many abilities. He had always known that his uncontrolled brutality was not something he liked, but it was not in the man to apologize afterward. It was also not in him to say the three words so needed by his children—I love you! He wondered if all the brutality would have stopped if he had faced him down years before. But given the viciousness of the last beating he had witnessed his oldest brother receive, as long as he had been physically weaker, he had always been afraid of getting crippled or even killed. He would never know for sure, but now it was over, finally and completely.

The last faint hope of a relationship between father and son faded with the sound of Carl's receding footsteps down the stairway. Michael would struggle for decades to come with resentment and outright hatred over the violence in his upbringing. When peace and true forgiveness finally came, it would be incredibly liberating! But the many years between now and then would be marked by hurts, resentment, frustration, and even hate. Although in the coming years, he tried various times to open up to churchgoing men and even ministers about his frustrations, he was always rebuffed and several times, criticized. It was much easier for them to believe that a boy would make up stories than that a man they knew as affable and humorous would abuse his kids!

# RANDY TIES THE KNOT

The next few weeks were a blur of activity with wedding preparations and work on the house. Michael and Randy's relationship had been close since childhood, but it seemed extra tight now. They had their differences and disagreements, but they were closer in age than any of the other brothers. Randy had been born in October of 1953, and Michael had come along eighteen months later in May of 1955. Since Charlotte always maintained that she had never had two babies in diapers at the same time, Randy proudly claimed that he had been potty-trained at eighteen months. It wasn't the type of accomplishment that gets one a bronze engraved plaque to hang on the wall in a prominent location, but it was something! They shared a lot of the same interests, but Randy's interest in sporty cars had waned after feeding his fuel-hungry 442 Oldsmobile for a few years. Michael recognized that muscle cars were an enormous drag on limited financial resources, but to him, the heady feeling of cruising down the road with all that power under you was worth the expense.

Money management in the Raptor family was basically an unlearned skill. Charlotte had always had the ability to stretch a dollar to cover about five dollars' worth of need when money was scarce. But when money was a bit more abundant, she was not afraid to spend it. Neither Carl nor his wife presumed to teach their sons financial management. Except for the times when money was extremely scarce, it was not an issue in their household. It was viewed as a tool which they neither despised nor worshipped. While this attitude may have seemed ideal in some social sense, the osmosis of its effect on the next generation was rather sad. While all of the boys would venture into their own businesses at least one time in their adult lives, none of them became financial success stories.

Michael, who would spend most of his adult life managing his own business, often wished that someone had instilled in him the importance of money in life and especially in business. He ran his business more for the freedom it afforded him, coupled with his love for building things, than for financial gain. In time, he came to realize his areas of weakness, of which his lack of drive for financial wealth was arguably his greatest. He saw that same monetary malaise in his brothers. While the Bible warns many times about the danger of loving money, he came to believe he had the opposite problem.

Money is such a huge part of peoples' daily existence that too often it becomes their focus and the main object of their desire. Some religious orders recognize the dangers of their congregants getting wrapped up in and controlled by money and make rules for their members governing its use. There are no rules, however, limiting the flow of cash into (ahem...) the offering plate.

Michael often wished for and even prayed many times for more appreciation for money. He had always had the ability to earn good wages, and he enjoyed spending it as much as the next person, but he had no vision of saving or accumulating it for the future. He had always been turned off by financially hard-up people trying to look spiritual because of their poverty. He had seen people who glorified their poverty, laugh with their hands over their mouths to hide their bad teeth. Some of them tore old clothes into squares to use for handkerchiefs.

Eventually Michael took a course offered by the famous Dave Ramsey on finances. In the course of the teaching, Dave held up a brick for the audience to see. "Money," he said, "is like this brick. I can use this brick to build a beautiful building or I can use it to smash a window. What I choose to do with the brick is not the fault of the brick. It does not make it good or bad. The brick is only a tool in my hand."

There has always been a popular theory that most people will live at approximately the same economic plane as they were raised in. While that theory often seems to hold true, there are always some who, through either hard work or good fortune, manage to take their economic standings to a higher level. There are also some who through sloth, addictions, or ill fortune, slide to a lower standard of living. On balance, everyone's quality of life becomes the sum total of the decisions they make and the effort they expend reaching goals.

The big day finally arrived for Randy and Maria's wedding. Randy had let Michael know that he had no problem with people decorating the honeymoon chariot, so Michael and his buddies decided they would not disappoint him. The chapel where they were married was only several blocks from her parents' house, and the little Vega was stashed inside their garage. When the festivities began to wind down, Michael, Nate, and Lane slipped into the garage and began to decorate the car with tin cans tied to the bumper, streamers from the roof, and soaped messages on the windows. When they had finished, they were rather proud of their handiwork and returned to the reception to help with cleanup.

It was customary for all family members and good friends to gather to see the bridal couple off on their honeymoon, so Michael returned to the garage to find some very irate church matrons scrubbing their handiwork off the Vega before Randy even saw it. Maria's brother was a preacher in their church, and his wife was leading the pack of female do-gooders. When she saw Michael and his friends, she loudly proclaimed before all present that this was a terrible testimony to any neighbors who saw it and that "this type of thing should *never* happen in our churches!" By the time the happy couple left for their wedding night, the car was freshly washed, and the offending decorations had been consigned to the dumpster. Unfortunately, Randy had recently had the car painted, and it had been a cheap paint job. Some of the soap writings had absorbed into the paint and could not be removed. He and Maria graciously forgave the offenders for their misdeeds. It was not quite so easy for the offended sister-in-law!

# TIME TO LEAVE

It was time for Michael to leave home. Nate was also experiencing turbulence at home, and they began to plan where to go together. By now, they were inseparable, and it was a given that whatever they did they would do together. Michael really wanted Nate to come back to Pennsylvania with him, but Nate was not interested in the area or the whole new set of people. He had relatives in northern Indiana, and they had all enjoyed it there, so they decided to go there and look for work. Neither of them had any significant funds to draw from, but Nate managed to borrow several hundred dollars from his father, and Michael gathered what he could come up with. They took only the Nova SS and enough clothes and supplies for a couple weeks. The plan was to find jobs, rent an apartment together, and live the good life. If they could land jobs in the high-paying RV factories, they would have plenty of money to enjoy life and their muscle cars.

There were no goodbyes as Michael prepared to leave head out the door with his suitcases. Instead, before he left, his mother pointedly instructed him not to forget to send money home to them. Michael shot her a perplexed look. He could see absolutely no reason why he should send his money home when he was permanently gone. They all knew he would never be back, and how long did they expect him to give them his money? "I don't think I will be doing that anymore," he said calmly. He saw her face tighten with anger as he picked up his suitcase and walked out to his waiting buddy.

Much later, Michael learned that this incident had indeed angered his parents. They reciprocated by giving each of the other children a nice amount of cash under the guise of returning money they had sent home. Michael never saw, however, the money he had sent home from his work in Pennsylvania.

Although the relationship between Michael and his parents would be strained throughout much of their lives, to their credit, their children were always welcome home for visits. Carl and Charlotte were always good hosts to their children's friends, who in turn tended to think they were great parents. While Michael knew it would never work to attempt to live at home again, he also knew the door would always be open to visit. But at the ripe old age of eighteen and with great friends to hang out with, the future was bright, and the whole world was open before him. And there was a very good-looking black-haired girl who lived in Northern Indiana who he would really like to get to know better.

Nate's enthusiasm was obvious as he opened his trunk to receive Michael's bags, then closed it with a solid *thunk*, and climbed behind the wheel. The Nova SS was gleaming in the morning sun, with little reflections flashing off his new mag wheels. The trend was to jack up cool cars and install wide tires with some type of chrome wheels. The cars' mufflers were exchanged for customized units which were much louder and emitted a crackling sound, especially on downshift. The practical fact that these modifications made the cars noisy, rough-riders was not a consideration. More changes were straight ahead in their immediate futures. They would become known in Indiana as "the Ohio boys" and were welcomed by most of the young ladies, while many of the young men would have preferred if they had stayed in Ohio! Michael could not know it now, but while the next two years would definitely not be problem-free, they would be the best two years of his life. He would come to develop great friendships with many more guys, but there would never have a closer friend than the fun-loving blond kid behind the wheel of his rumbling Nova headed south.

# EPILOGUE

They arrived in Wakarusa, Indiana, as the sun was about to disappear over the western horizon. Their new friend Larry had invited them to stay with them until they found jobs and an apartment, and he graciously shared his small rented bedroom with them. The young Mennonite couple he was boarding with had left the hybrid Amish-Mennonite church where Larry's father was the bishop and the three ordained leaders ruled with an iron fist. The church was rather new and mostly populated by zealous younger families. The price for the expression of much of this zeal was borne by the children and young people. Larry's home had turned into a virtual war zone, and while he had escaped relatively unscathed, his more volatile younger brother was embroiled in an ongoing battle worthy of Robert E. Lee!

Some of the stories that drifted out of that church almost made Michael shudder. The leaders had invited a preacher from another state to come and hold meetings. The preacher was a rabid supporter of beating children as punishment. He emphasized scriptural references like Proverbs 22:15, Proverbs 23:13–14, and Proverbs 19:18 where one of the admonitions is to "spare not for his crying" and "he shall not die." He recommended that rather than spank your child until he cries, you should "spank" them until they stop crying. After all, in the ancient nation of Israel, rebellious children were to be stoned to death!

One of the young fathers was known for his extreme spankings on his preschool children. Their church had a basement with several large support beams overhead. This man kept a wooden paddle on top of one of these beams, and the slightest infractions by his small children would earn them a trip to the basement where the other children could hear the smack of the paddle on flesh and the screams of the "disciplined" child.

One day, two of the younger boys discovered the paddle while they were playing in the basement and came up with the idea of driving some very small nails through it both directions. Their motivation was unclear, but it may have been to send a message to the young father. Unfortunately, the young father was worked up into such a state that he grabbed the paddle and began beating his child before he noticed the nails!

The next day, Nate and Michael began their earnest search for employment. Larry had given them a list of suggestions where to apply, and they drove from business to business putting in applications. But in spite of their construction backgrounds, no one seemed willing to hire a couple footloose out-of-state kids with no local address or phone. Over the next few days, they checked back as instructed, but in spite of a good economy, no jobs were available for them. After a couple days, they became embarrassed to keep hanging out in Larry's small room, so they kept their things in Nate's car and began sleeping in parking lots overnight.

Their concern grew as the end of the week approached and their funds continued to dwindle. They began to discuss going back home, but they both knew that would not be a long-term solution. However, they could not go on like this much longer. "I would say we give it until Monday, and if we don't find anything by then, we will head back to Ohio," Nate opined. Michael agreed, and they decided to enjoy the weekend in spite of their concerns.

They had been visiting the less conservative Salisbury Mennonite Church where Larry was attending, and it seemed to be a good option for them if they stayed around here. Michael was feeling a bit sick about the possibility of having to go home in defeat. He had every intention of moving back to Pennsylvania to stay if Indiana did not work out. The frustrating thing was that while he and Nate could pick up just about any job available back home, none of these hundreds of businesses around here seemed to want them.

Monday morning found the Ohio boys checking back with every business that had seemed at all hopeful, as well as a few additional ones, but the answer was always the same. There were no jobs to be had. The local factories were hiring dozens of brain-addled druggies every day, but they would not take a chance on a couple clean-looking young fellows with years of construction experience! That evening, two dejected young men looked up Larry and told him that they were out of options. They had to return home before their money ran out.

Larry was incredulous when he heard their tale of woe! "That's crazy!" he exclaimed. "These factories are hiring every day! Wait one more day and let me talk to my plant superintendent, John. He attends the conservative Mennonite church in the area, and he is very influential. I *know* he can get you jobs!"

"Okay," they agreed, "we will give it another day."

To their amazement, Larry had good news for them the following evening. John had agreed to interview them, and if they suited him, he would find them both factory jobs at his company called Holiday Rambler. This was one of the business that were manufacturing recreational vehicles, and they had grown rapidly to become one of the largest in the area. They were known for paying employees well. Michael, who had worked his way up to two dollars and seventy-five cents per hour, was astonished to hear that Larry was earning over five dollars per hour!

The next evening as instructed, Nate and Michael arrived at John's house for the interview. John was an obvious leader of men with a forceful personality which intimidated Michael enormously. Nate, however, seemed a little more at ease, and his father being a bishop in another conservative Mennonite church seemed to be a big factor in their favor. John asked them a number of questions about their backgrounds and whether their parents knew what they were doing then said he would see what he could find for them. He was as good as his word, and before the week was out, he had secured them both jobs in the cabinet shops at different plants. The plants were close enough together that they could ride together. Michael's starting pay would be three dollars and seventy-five cents per hour, and Nate's was to be four dollars and twenty-five cents per hour.

With a huge sense of relief, they began to search for an affordable apartment. They found a two-bedroom, upstairs apartment at a price they could manage, but the deposit left them very little for food and gas money. But they were not about to complain. This was the beginning of a whole new life in a completely different world. And the future had never looked brighter to Michael Raptor!